D1206947

THE POETIC JESUS

BY ANDREW YOUNG

Collected Poems, Hart-Davis

Nicodemus: a Mystery, with incidental music by Imogen Holst, Cape

A Prospect of Flowers, Cape

A Retrospect of Flowers, Cape

A Prospect of Britain, Hutchinson

THE POETIC JESUS

ANDREW YOUNG

WITH
SIX WOOD ENGRAVINGS
BY
T. R. WILLIAMS

LONDON

S·P·C·K

1972

First published in 1972 by S.P.C.K.
Holy Trinity Church, Marylebone Road
London NW1 4DU

Printed in Great Britain by
William Clowes & Sons, Limited
London, Beccles and Colchester

SBN 281 02628 9

THE POETIC JESUS

is based on the Synoptic Gospels, but borrows from the Fourth Gospel the correct date for the institution of the Last Supper. Some modern scholars regard certain sayings in the Synoptics as too poetical not to have been the invention of the early Church; the title *The Poetic Jesus* suggests that the opposite of that is the case.

Jesus, Greek transcript for Joshua, God Saves, was a common name; several High Priests had the name; but it fell into disuse, hated by Jews, while held in too great reverence by Christians. He had no surname, but came to be called Mk 6.3
"the carpenter's son" or "the Nazarene". Though his birth- Mt 2.23
day, Christmas, has been so widely and joyfully celebrated, we do not know its date; probably it was about 6 B.C. It was fitting it should have inspired two of the world's most poetic stories: one about shepherds keeping watch over their flock by night, an unlikely thing to do, if Christmas was in winter; the other about wise men, astrologers, who followed a star, a story that may owe something to Balaam's prophetic poem about a divine king:

> There shall come a star out of Jacob, Num 24.17
> and a sceptre shall rise out of Israel.

But his birthday also inspired a poem, the *Song of Zacharias* or the *Benedictus*. It tells of a sunrise, its light not ascending from earth's horizon to heaven, but descending from heaven to earth:

Lk 1.68–79 The dayspring from on high hath visited us
to give light to them that sit in darkness,
and in the shadow of death.

Yet this celebrated Child was brought up in a humble way.
When forty days after his birth he was dedicated in the
Holy Temple in Jerusalem, only a pair of young pigeons
Lk 2.24 was sacrificed, a poor thank-offering; most people aimed at
a lamb, as prescribed by the Law.

Nazareth had a few good houses; they were at the foot of
the High Street by the fountain from which Mary carried
water each morning, later called the Virgin's Well. But
most of the houses were poor, their walls made of sun-
baked bricks of mud and straw. A burglar could break into
an empty house at night. Perhaps the memory of such a
case, the talk of the little town in his boyhood, suggested
Lk 12.39 years later the saying, "If the goodman of the house had
known what hour the thief would come, he would have
watched and not suffered his house to be dug through." For
the saying is odd, at least its application: "Be ye therefore
Lk 12.40 ready, for the Son of Man cometh in an hour when ye think
not." He compared himself to a burglar!

The house had one room; the lamp set on the lamp-
Mt 5.15 stand, not as in daytime under a meal-tub, gave light to all
in the house. Later he spoke of the scribes and Pharisees
hiding their lamp under a meal-tub, God's revelation of
himself overshadowed by the Law elaborated with endless
rules and regulations. The room was small; Joseph could
Lk 11.5f have been the man who, lying in bed with his children,
spoke through the closed door with a neighbour begging
three loaves of bread for an unexpected guest. There was
no window; the lamp did not cast a patch of light on "the

outer darkness". But there was a closet; it was used as a
store-room, but he came to think the best use for such a
place was for saying a prayer. "Shut the door of thy closet; Mt 6.6
thy Father which seeth in secret shall reward thee openly."
An outside staircase led to a flat roof made of branches
spread on crossbeams and covered with straw and lime. It
was by such a staircase his friends were to bring a paralytic
boy and, making a hole, lower him into the crowded room Mk 2.4
to be healed. The incident was to cause great offence, not
because plaster fell on the heads of the crowd, but because
he said, "Son, thy sins are forgiven thee." Though he healed
the boy, who was he, a sinner himself, to assume the office
of God?

The small one-roomed house gave him a close view of
Mary's domestic work. He remembered her throwing salt
out in the street. Severely taxed, salt was not cheap, but
coming mostly from the Dead Sea, called also the Salt Sea,
it was apt to lose its savour. That lost, he was to say to his
disciples, "it is fit for nothing but to be cast out and trodden Mt 5.13
under foot of men". He watched Mary baking bread in the
mud-oven; she mixed leaven with the meal and worked it
with her fingers till the lump was in commotion with
rising bubbles. He remembered it when he began his
ministry; his proclamation of the coming Kingdom worked Mt 13.33
like leaven in the listening crowds, stirring them with a like
commotion. With six or seven children growing up Mary
must have wondered if it was not worth while to patch old Mk 2.21
garments; of course the patch might come away, leaving
the rent worse. He was not to have a like wonder about his
teaching; while John the Baptist's teaching was a patch on
the old religion of the scribes and Pharisees, his Gospel was
a whole new garment. Or, as he was to see it in another

Mk 2.22 picture, it was not like new wine put into old leather
bottles, wine that still fermenting caused the shrunk
bottles to burst. Perhaps he remembered hearing in his
Nazareth home a bottle bursting with a bang, That, of
course, would have been Joseph's fault, not Mary's.

Most people in Palestine were poor, salt only one of many
things heavily taxed; they were doubly taxed themselves,
by the Roman and Temple authorities. If, as is likely,
Lk 15.8 Mary was the woman who, having lost a silver coin, swept
the whole house, the room's rush-covered floor, and, having
found it, called in her friends and neighbours, saying,
"Rejoice with me", to her and her husband a small coin
was a large sum of money. Probably they could afford meat
only for the Sabbath supper, cooked of course on Friday,
the day before. Coneys and hares were common creatures,
but like swine they were unclean, fit only for foxes. The
Boy knew the price of the cheapest food sold in the market,
Mt 10.29 his mother sending him to buy it, two sparrows sold for a
farthing and, one thrown into the bargain, five sparrows
Lk 12.6 sold for two farthings. But Galilee was famous for its corn,
and if the Boy asked for bread, he would not have been
Mt 7.9 given—a stone. The Lake of Galilee abounded with fish; if
they could be exported to Alexandria, even to Rome, they
would reach Nazareth; and if the Boy asked for a fish, he
Mt 7.10 would not be given—a serpent. The terraced hills round
Nazareth rich in fruit-trees, figs, and pomegranates were
cheap. And there was wine; it was so plentiful that grapes
were used as raisins. And every Sabbath morning Joseph
offered a prayer which began, "Blessed art thou, O Lord
our God, king of the universe, who createst the fruit of the
vine". But whatever its conditions, the Boy grew up with a
happy, even holy, experience of his home. The familiar
Mk 14.36 word with which he addressed Joseph, Abba, Dear Father,
was the word with which he came to address God.

Joseph taught the Boy the Jewish Creed, the Shema, the "Hear"; Shema is Hebrew for Hear, as Credo is Latin for Creed; "Hear, O Israel, the Lord thy God is one Lord". He had to recite it morning and evening. No doubt Joseph also taught him a few passages of Holy Scripture. Though the *Psalms* were not yet strictly a part of the Canon, the *Twenty-third Psalm*, "The Lord is my shepherd", would no doubt suggest itself. He would be told by Joseph that it was written by King David, at one time himself a shepherd; to inherit doubtful or mistaken information was implied in his Incarnation. Deut 6.4 Mk 12.29

At the age of five or six he went to school, education being compulsory. "Our chief care is to educate our children well," said Josephus; it has been claimed that Jews were better educated than Greeks. The school, attached to the synagogue, was a church school. The master was the minister or his deacon; pupils sat about him in a semicircle on the floor. Of the games he played with his fellow-pupils, and with the girls, we know of only two, marriages and funerals. Perhaps the married couple were boy and girl; for a funeral a dead mouse would serve, or even a grass-hopper. The girls played on pipes and the boys danced as men did at a wedding; then the boys moaned and the girls wailed like women hired to wail at a funeral. The two parties did not always play harmoniously:

> We have piped unto you,
> and ye have not danced; Mt 11.16–19
> We have mourned unto you.
> and ye have not lamented.

The little poem expresses what he felt afterwards, the frivolous, perverse attitude of people to the preaching of himself and John the Baptist, the one glad tidings, the other a doleful judgement. It is pleasant to think that, thanks to him, that venerable book, the Holy Bible, has a reminiscence of children's games.

At school he learned to read and write, but his main study was the Law, the first five books of Holy Scripture. Law sounds a hard study for a boy, but the greatest law, "Thou shalt love thy neighbour as thyself", is not very
Lev 19.18 legal. He would learn it by heart, but not the law that
strangely follows it, "Thou shalt not wear a garment of
Lev 19.19 mingled linen and wool". And the Law had many interest-
Gen 3.1 ing stories, from the serpent speaking to Eve in the garden
Num 22.28 to the ass speaking to Balaam in the vineyard. And it is
rich in poetry. It opens with a poem,

Gen 1.3 God said, let there be light,
and there was light,

lines quoted by Longinus as an instance of the Sublime. The teacher could not have failed to speak of a poem attributed to Moses, so great a lawyer that he was said to have left a precept for each day of the year. The poem relates how the Lord rescued Israel from Egypt:

As the eagle stirreth her nest,
Deut 32.11 and fluttereth over her young:
Spreadeth her wings and taketh them,
and beareth them on her wings.

The Boy's thoughts would take a far flight from sparrows sold two for a farthing to the Eagle bearing the Twelve Tribes on outspread wings.

About the age of twelve the Boy began the study of the

Prophets, which included the historical books of Scripture. These contain many poems, whole or in part.

> Sun, stand thou still on Gibeon, Josh 10.12
> and, thou, moon, in the valley of Ajalon,

is a sublime invocation to which an unpoetical editor added, "And the sun stood still". Of peculiar interest was the prophet Jonah. Though he was swallowed by a whale, his grave was not in the whale's belly; it was five miles from Nazareth. The Boy persuaded Joseph to take him there, for it was much frequented by pilgrims. Gazing at it in awe,
he was very far from saying, "Behold, a greater than Mt 12.41
Jonah is here". But the spiritual distance may have been a little lessened by the book itself, the most humanitarian in Scripture, perhaps in all literature, if a scholar could say, "I cannot even now take up this marvellous book, or even speak of it, without the tears rising to my eyes and my heart beating faster". The Boy may have wondered about the closing words spoken by the Lord, "and should not I
have pity on Nineveh, that great city, wherein are more Jonah 4.11
than sixscore thousand persons who cannot discern between the right hand and left"; who were the persons so blind? Told by the teacher they were little children, a tiny seed may have dropped in his mind that in time sprang up and produced a flower new in the world, a love of children other than parental.

Another prophet who interested the Boy was Hosea, the teacher having pointed out he was a namesake, Jesus and Hosea both being forms of Joshua. Jonah composed a poem in the whale's belly, the worst poem in Holy Scripture; Hosea was the most lyrical of all the prophets. He is called a Minor Prophet and, though that only means that he wrote a small book, the name seems wrong. Moving passages like the Lord's lament over his fallen people:

Hos 6.4 O Ephraim, how shall I give thee up?
O Israel, how shall I let thee go?
Thy goodness is as a morning mist,
as dew that early passes away,

may have helped to bring to birth even in the schoolboy the Poetic Jesus.

At six o'clock on Friday evening the double blast of a horn sounded from the flat roof of the synagogue master's house; the Sabbath had begun. As a new year began in
Gen 1.5 autumn, a new day began in the evening; "the evening and morning were the first day", says the Book of Genesis. While Mary stayed at home with his brothers and sisters, the Boy accompanied Joseph to the synagogue. They followed the practice of approaching it at a brisk pace, while on coming away they walked as with a slow reluctance. The exiled Jews in Babylonia, deprived of their Temple, built the first synagogues. Their form of worship popular, synagogues spread after the Exile throughout Palestine. If ten men in a small village promised to support a synagogue, it was built. They gained importance by the front facing the Holy Temple in Jerusalem. Though Nazareth was a little town, not mentioned in any writing before the Gospels, the Boy and Joseph were proud that it had a painted portico. Of course, it was humble compared with the synagogue in prosperous Capernaum, which with its rows of pillars looked like a temple to Jupiter.

As the synagogue was the prototype of the Christian Church, their services were similar, two lessons, psalms, prayers, and a sermon. The lessons were from the Law and the Prophets, written on separate scrolls; they were read in Hebrew and then translated into Aramaic. This would be

the beginning of the Boy's knowledge of Hebrew. On Passover Sabbath there was a special lesson from the *Song of* 1 Kings 4.32
Songs. It was attributed to Solomon; "His songs were a thousand and five", but this was his masterpiece. A collection of love lyrics, if such it is, it had taken on a religious character. The Lord lovingly asked of his chosen and peculiar people,

> Who is she that looketh forth as the morning, Song of Solomon 6.10
> fair as the moon, clear as the sun,
> and terrible as an army with banners?

As the title *Song of Songs* means the world's best poem, the poetic Boy may have owed more to it than to *Hosea*.

He had other education than the synagogue with its school could provide. Galilee of the Nations, as the country was called, was widely open to foreigners, to Romans, and even more to Greeks. Most Galileans would know a little Latin.
"Whosoever shall compel thee to go a mile, go with him Mt 5.41
twain"; a Roman soldier, ordering a Jew to carry his kit, would be less likely to speak Aramaic than the Jew to understand Latin. Three of his disciples were to have Greek names, Andrew meaning manly, Philip a horse-lover, and Peter a rock, a name that gave rise to the famous pun,
"Thou art Peter, and on this rock I will build my church". Mt 16.18
Nazareth itself was a little out-of-the-way town, so that "Can Jn 1.46
there any good thing come of Nazareth?" was asked. The High Street was an answer; from the Fountain of the Virgin it climbed through the town to become a track leading to a small hill-top on the surrounding ridge. It was the high
mountain to which Satan took him later to view the whole Mt 4.8
world. From the tropical Jordan Valley, deep beneath sea-level, to Mount Hermon with its patches of summer snow

2 Sam 23.20 there was every variety of climate. "Benaiah slew a lion on
a day of snow." And the scene was full of the history that
mattered most to a Jew; from the Valley of Jezreel rose the
Judg 7 hill of Moreh where Gideon defeated the Moabites and
1 Sam 31 Mount Gilboa where the Philistines defeated Saul. Round
the foot of the mountainous little hill-top ran the world's
greatest road, paved white by the Romans, the caravan
route from Egypt to Damascus and the Orient, while in the
distance shone its greatest waterway, the Mediterranean
Jonah 1.17 Sea, where a whale swallowed Jonah on his way to Spain.
There was no need for the Boy to see Rome; of that imperial
city he saw enough in a soldier who might order him to
carry his kit. The track to the hill-top he must often have
taken, returning from a view of the world to sleepy
Nazareth to dream dreams and see visions. Even then he
may have had a vision of what was much greater than the
world, and much less, the Kingdom of God.

The country about Nazareth had not the bare, stony look
it had later; it received more of that gift bestowed by God
Mt 5.45 on the just and the unjust, rain. At times the gift seemed
too generous; hills were terraced to prevent their earth
being washed away. But the terraces became rich in fruit-
trees and flowers; "Galilee appears to be one great garden",
said Josephus. And the general soil was productive. There
were a few farmers with slaves, but most of it was cultivated
by smallholders. They would often need the carpenter of
Nazareth. Sometimes he took with him the Boy to learn
the business he was likely to inherit. And the Boy was glad
to go. He was interested in the smallholder's labours, for
later they provided him with allegoric pictures. "No man,
Lk 9.62 having put his hand to the plough and looking back, is fit
for the Kingdom of God." The wooden plough had a single
shaft, held by the ploughman's right hand, a leather thong
in his left; as it was commonly drawn by two animals of

different strength, as an ox and an ass, to drive a straight furrow he could not afford to turn his head. "The Son of
Man shall separate the sheep from the goats, setting the Mt 25.33
sheep on his right hand, but the goats on his left." In the daytime they usually made one flock, but in the evening they were put in different folds, the goats' fold often a cave; that the sheep were the more valuable, providing wool as well as milk, and also because the goats were black, was why the Judge put the sheep on his right hand and the goats on his left. The Poetic Jesus had his roots in the earth.

But if the Boy was interested in smallholders' labours, his eyes were open to God's works. Being the Boy he was, there was for him no such thing as "dead nature". Already he had begun to feel about sky and earth what he expressed later in his saying,

> Swear not by heaven, Mt 5.34–5
> for it is God's throne;
> Nor by the earth,
> for it is his footstool.

Joseph's death roused him from any dreams inspired by the prospect of the wide world from the little hill-top behind Nazareth; he was the bread-winner of the family, a carpenter.

> Why behold the chip in thy brother's eye, Mt 7.3
> and consider not the beam in your own eye?

suggests a carpenter with a grim sense of humour. But work in the little town, though it included making coffins, would not give him full employment, and he followed Joseph's steps in going far afield, fashioning ploughs and yokes for smallholders. That he did his work well is unconsciously suggested in the saying,

Mt 11.29 Take my yoke upon you,
 and learn of me;
For my yoke is easy,
 and my burden is light,

a saying not suggesting that it is easy to be a good Christian, but that his teaching fitted human nature better, and was less of a burden, than the elaborated Law of the scribes and Pharisees.

But Galilee abounded more in stone than in wood, and "carpenter" meant less a worker in wood than a stonemason. He was to show an unusual interest in that hard
Ps 118.22 element. He himself was a stone, the stone which the build-
Mt 21.42 ers rejected, though it was to become the head of the
Mt 7.24 corner; his teaching was a rock on which a wise man would build his house so that it would not be swept away by a winter flood like a house built on sand. That he was a stone-mason as well as a worker in wood is supported by a saying attributed to him in an Egyptian papyrus:

Raise the stone,
 and thou shalt find me;
Cleave the wood,
 and there am I.

The saying has been considered authentic for several reasons, but not for the most likely, that it is very poetical.

Even when working on a stone sepulchre, the Carpenter may have allowed his thoughts to wander. What Greeks and Romans looked back on, Jews looked forward to, a Golden Age. Though none of the prophets had expressly spoken of it, people's minds were full of a Coming Kingdom. It would be a glorification of Israel, established on Mount Zion. One poetic prophet saw rocky Jerusalem like a city on the Euphrates or the Nile, protected by the river and canals:

> There the glorious Lord will be unto us Isa 33.21
> a place of broad rivers and streams;
> Wherein shall go no galley with oars,
> neither shall gallant ship pass thereby.

It would be a time of great prosperity,

> a feast of fat things, Isa 25.6
> a feast of wine on the lees.

Proselytes flowing into it from all nations, it would be a time of peace;

> They shall beat their swords into ploughshares, Isa 2.4
> their spears into pruning-hooks.

But God would first punish his sinful people: "Behold, the Mal 4.1
day cometh that shall burn as an oven." So said the last of the prophets, significantly called Malachi, My Messenger. But four and a half centuries had passed; earlier enemies had not beaten their swords into ploughshares, and now the Romans were far from beating their spears into pruning-hooks. But the Lord would send his Messiah, the Anointed; he would restore his chosen people and establish a new Davidic Kingdom.

> Blessed be the Lord God of Israel, Lk 1.68
> for he hath visited and redeemed his people,

sang Zacharias in a Nativity Canticle. His Kingdom would be supreme among the nations, yet embracing proselytes

Lk 2.32 a light to lighten the Gentiles,
and the glory of thy people Israel,

sang Simeon in another Canticle.

Already a Messiah had appeared, Judas. The Carpenter remembered his revolt, for it had taken place near Nazareth, when he was a boy. Though it was crushed and was followed by crucifixions, the land became alive with zealots, more in Galilee than elsewhere. They so looked for their conquering Davidic king that, as he said of them later,

Mt 11.12 The Kingdom of Heaven suffereth violence,
and the violent take it by force.

His sympathy was more with the scribes and Pharisees, whose Messiah would come in clouds of glory and, though Prince of Peace, would sweep away the power of Rome with his breath, and establish a kingdom true to its name Israel, God Reigns. Perhaps it would be the prelude to a new Aeon, of an other-worldly character, in which all tragic human history would come to an end. God would be prompted to act by the people's obedience to the Law. How sacred was the Law, two thousand years older than the world, studied by God Himself. If for two Sabbaths the people kept the Law strictly, the Messiah would come. The Carpenter often wondered about the expected Messiah, as though with a personal interest.

Yet it was less the Messiah people looked for than a
herald of the Kingdom; "Behold I send you Elijah the Mal 4.5
prophet". But was he not already come in a man, John,
surnamed the Baptist because of a water-rite. Baptism was
in use in Judaea; it changed a Gentile into a Jew, making
him so completely another man that, as was argued, he
could marry his sister or even his mother. John's baptism
was a propitiatory preparation for the Judgement which
would precede the Kingdom. He was a herald proclaiming
the coming of one whose shoe's-latchet he was not worthy Mk 1.7
to unloose. And he looked like Elijah who, caught up to
heaven alive, had returned to earth. He, too, lived in the
wilderness, as it was called, the country about the Jordan
River and the Dead Sea, and like Elijah he wore a cloak of
camel's hair, held by a leather girdle, and fasted on locusts Mk 1.6
and wild honey. From Jerusalem and all Judaea people
thronged to the preaching of John and, though some said
"He hath a devil", most were thrilled by his proclamation
and submitted to the water-rite. Even from distant
Capernaum a caravan set out each week for the Jordan
Valley.

Though he heard John's voice calling him from the wilderness, he waited till James, his eldest brother, was

able to support the fatherless family. He was then about
thirty years of age. The wilderness, though called in
Num 21.20 Scripture Jeshimon, Desolation, was not an empty desert.
It was full of history; there the Lord had by a deed of
Ex 4.22 covenant made Israel his chosen people: "Israel is my son,
my firstborn." Yet it was full of dead men; of all who had
escaped from Egypt, crossing the Red Sea, only two had
reached the Land of Promise, Joshua, son of Nun, and
Num 14.30 Caleb, son of Jephunneh. What was going to be his own
experience? He found John not far from where the Jordan
buries itself without resurrection in its deep grave, the
Dead Sea. He had a small band of disciples with whom he
shared a private prayer. He was no river-reed, obsequious
Mt 11.7 to the wind. Strangely inspired by the snakes and stones of
Mt 3.7 the wilderness, "O generation of vipers", he addressed
some Pharisees, and to the crowd who trusted they were
true Israelites he said that God was able from the stones to
Mt 3.9 raise children to Abraham. As for the Coming one, he
Mt 3.11 would be a Judge baptizing with fire. John's baptizing with
water was in the hope it would put out the fire. The
Mt 3.12 Coming One would also be a smallholder who, winnowing-
fan in hand, would toss from the threshing-floor the mingled grain and chaff to be separated in the evening wind; the
wheat he would gather in his garner, the chaff he would
burn with fire. The Carpenter did not see himself as a
smallholder.

To a baptism, the sign of repentance, he might not have
submitted himself but for another prophet's picture of the
Isa 53.12 Coming One, "numbered with the transgressors". Perhaps
he hesitated, and then took the plunge, slowly wading into
Isa 64.1 the Jordan. "Oh that thou wouldest rend the heavens and
come down", that other prophet had prayed. And so it
happened. As he raised his head out of the water, "He saw
the heavens rending", all seven of them, "and the Spirit

like a dove descending upon him; and there was a voice Mk 1.10
from heaven saying, thou art my beloved son, in whom I
am well pleased". So later he described his experience to
his disciples, perhaps after their visit to Caesarea Philippi.
They took his oriental poetry literally; he had seen a vision
and heard a voice. They may have noticed that in his quotation from a Psalm "Thou art my son" he added "beloved"; Ps 2.7
but perhaps they missed the significance of the intimate
"dove"; the Holy Spirit, brooding upon the face of the
chaotic waters at creation and calming them, was pictured
as that peaceful bird, a dove.

"He was in all points tempted like as we are." Perhaps he Heb 4.15
was, but he was also tempted unlike as we are. He remembered that "Thou art my son" is followed in the Psalm with
"Ask of me, and I shall give thee the heathen for thine Ps 2.8
inheritance". He was called to undertake a world-wide
mission, to establish God's Kingdom on earth. Our temptations are personal, his were official. "And immediately the
Spirit driveth him into the wilderness." We are drawn to Mk 1.12
our temptations, not driven to them by the Spirit.

He climbed from the Jordan to where the wilderness
looks down on the Dead Sea, and falls to it in blasted rock,
an awe-inspiring place. He felt the need to be alone, or as he
later put it, "alone, yet not alone, for the Father is with Jn 16.32
me". But he had worse company; "he was with the beasts", Mk 1.13
creatures associated with demons. Vultures sailing overhead and jackals gazing at the strange phenomenon, a man,
no place could have been more unlike the Garden of Eden;
yet he had it mind when in his figurative way he described his experience to his disciples. As Satan came to the
Garden of Eden to tempt Eve, so he came to the wilderness
to tempt him. Eve was tempted to eat an apple, he to

change stones into bread. Both temptations were very
tempting; Eve would become an enlightened woman; he
would become a great benefactor, using his gifts to change
an impoverished people into a prosperous. Overtaxed by
Rome, many were looking for such a benefactor in the
promised Messiah. But he did not see himself as an in-
surgent patriot or even as a politician. His mission and gifts
Mt 4.4 were spiritual, and "Man does not live by bread alone"
he sharply said to Satan. So he told his disciples, continuing
to speak of his experience in a picturesque way.

But Satan presented him with a much grander picture
than a prosperous Israel, God's people exalted above the
nations with himself as Messianic King. He took him to an
exceeding high mountain, the little hill-top behind
Nazareth, from which he could view in a moment of time
Mt 4.9 the world's kingdoms and their wealth; "All these will I
give thee, if thou wilt fall down and worship me". Even as
a boy, returning from the hill-top with its wide prospect,
he had wondered what part he might play in the world.
He wondered about it much more when he remembered
"Thou art my son" is followed in the psalm "Ask of me,
and I shall give thee the heathen for thine inheritance, and
the uttermost parts of the earth for thy possession". But
could he ask that of his Father, whose will he was on earth
only to fulfil? The knowledge that he was God's Son made
him humble, not exalted. To entertain any ambition for
himself was to fall down and worship Satan. The poetic
way he described his experience may have made the disciples think that the Black One, as he was called, had
Mt 4.10 appeared in person to tempt him, and "Get thee behind
me, Satan" he had said.

As in the second temptation his memory went back to a
scene of his boyhood, so also in the third. At the age of
Lk 2.42 twelve he was taken to Jerusalem to become a Son of the

Law, a kind of confirmation. Joseph, showing him the Temple, pointed out a pinnacle on which it was popularly expected that at some Passover the Messiah, the Anointed would appear. If the words, "Thou art my son", meant that he was the Messiah, might he not stand on the pinnacle himself? But he imagined something more. Would not the people expect their Messiah to be a thaumaturge?
He was not wrong; "The Jews seek a sign", said St Paul, 1 Cor 1.22
who knew them well. More than once the Pharisees asked him to show them a sign. Even the wilderness whispered that Elijah had worked a wonder, dividing the water of the Jordan with his mantle. Satan suggested something more spectacular than a figure perched on a pinnacle. "If thou be the Son of God, cast thyself down; for it is written, he
shall give his angels charge concerning thee lest thou dash Mt 4.6–7
thy foot against a stone." But he could quote Scripture as well as Satan and replied, "It is also written, thou shalt not tempt the Lord thy God". The dramatic account of his temptations which he gave his disciples he ended with a significant little couplet,

Satan left me for a season Mt 4.11
and the angels came and ministered to me.

What the angels ministered to him was not water, but wine, the exhilarating faith that his temptation by Satan had confirmed his baptism by God. But they also gave him food for thought: how was he to fulfil his mission? John was his forerunner; he would follow his steps so far and be his own forerunner, proclaiming the Coming One; then he would overtake John, presenting himself as the One who was come. But he would not follow John into the wilderness; he would make Capernaum his headquarters. It was only a day's walk from Nazareth, and that it was named after

a prophet, Nahum, may have seemed significant. Perhaps
he was already familiar with the town. That he was later
addressed as "Rabbi, my Master", and that he had pupils,
his disciples, suggests he may have had a higher education
than the little synagogue at Nazareth could provide. There
were scholarships, and one may have taken him to the
synagogue school at Capernaum. In any case his forecast
Mt 9.1 that he would be closely associated with the town was
correct; it became "his own city".

Secluded on one side by a brown mountain-range, it was
open on the other side to the blue Sea of Galilee, which St
Luke, a foreigner familiar with the Mediterranean Sea,
calls a Lake. Perhaps it was neither sea nor lake, being about
seven hundred feet below sea-level. It had a Roman gar-
rison, for many of the Galileans were zealots; there was
also a custom-house on the caravan route to Damascus,
farmed out by the Roman authority to a publican named
Levi. "Village of Nahum", it had become a prosperous
town. It was famous for its fish; there is a reminiscence of
Mt 5.13 its fish-market in his many sayings about salt. But perhaps
he preferred to speak in the cornmarket, John having foretold that the Coming One would gather grain in his garner.
If the markets were sometimes crowded, there were fishing
villages along the coast. Also on the Sabbath there was the
synagogue, all the better for being crowded. If advanced
study had gained him the title, "Rabbi, my Master", he
would be invited to preach. Also he could obtain a lodging
in the town. It was considered meritorious in ladies,
especially in widows, to give hospitality to a Rabbi who
preached in the synagogue. Though compared with John,
who lived on locusts and wild honey, he was "a man
Mt 11.19 gluttonous and a wine-bibber", he would not be like the
Mt 23.14 Rabbis of whom he later said, "they devour widows'
houses".

The tetrarch, Herod Antipas, put John in a dungeon, alarmed by this proclamation of One so mighty that he was not worthy to be his slave. This new prophet, as people regarded him, presented no mighty appearance. He spoke little of himself, leaving his words to speak for him. But behind them was authority: "I am come that . . ." "I am sent that . . ." "Verily I say unto you . . ." "Ye have heard it said of old time, but I say . . .". Like John he called on people to repent. But while for John repentance meant only a sorrowful confession of sin, for him it was much more. A saying attributed to him is so strange that it is probably authentic: "Except ye make that which is upwards as that which downwards, and that which is before you as that which is behind, ye shall not know the Kingdom
of God." Repentance was a complete change of outlook,
and so of life. "There is joy among the angels in heaven Lk 15.7
over one sinner that repenteth", a birthday celebration.
"Except ye become as little children, ye shall not enter the Mt 18.3
Kingdom of Heaven." "Never man spake like this man", Jn 7.46
people said truly. But there was more. St Luke in the *Acts
of the Apostles* speaks of "all that Jesus began to do and to Acts 1.1
teach"; the order of words suggests that performance came before precept, that he himself practised what he preached. How heavenly a life he must have lived to be able to tell people to be perfect as their Father in Heaven was perfect.

One unique thing about him was that he attracted women and showed a love for their children. At a synagogue service women sat in an enclosed place at the back of the building, hardly part of the congregation; they would not have followed John into the wilderness, even though they could have been baptized; to this new Prophet mothers brought their children to be given his blessing. His followers rebuked them for interrupting a discourse,
but he rebuked them: "Suffer the little children to come Mk 10.14

unto me, for of such is the Kingdom of Heaven." St Mark
tells that twice he took a child in his arms, but the other
evangelists, though they wrote with his earlier Gospel
before them, omit to mention the acts; they added nothing
to the dignity of the Son of God. They were remembered,
however, by the early Church and gave rise to what otherwise might have seemed unpermissible, Infant Baptism.
Mt 18.10 A saying about "these little ones", "their angels do always
behold the face of my Father in heaven", has been misunderstood; it does not refer to "guardian angels"; it is an
anticipation by many centuries of Wordsworth's

> Heaven lies about us in our infancy,

and more poetical.

A sermon in the synagogue had an alarming interruption;
a man began shouting, "What have you to do with us,
Mk 1.24 Jesus of Nazareth?" The man was a demoniac. The world
was full of demons, haunting desert places, and also tombs,
where they were recruited by spirits of the dead. "The sons
Gen 6.2 of God saw the daughters of men, that they were fair, and
they took them wives"; demons were popularly supposed
to be their offspring. But as the *Book of Genesis* says their off-
Gen 6.4 spring were giants, it would seem more likely that demons
were the offspring of Adam's first wife, Lilith, herself a
demon. Certainly they were far from gigantic; they were
aerial enough to take possession of people, causing various
Lk 8.2 disorders. Mary Magdalene was possessed with seven
demons, almost the maximum number; though the name
"Magdalene" came to have a bad connotation, we do not
know their nature. A demon's action was obvious in an
epileptic falling to the ground with hand clutching the air.
Mk 7.32f When he healed a man with an impediment in his speech,

the string of his tongue was unloosed; who could have been holding it but a demon? He inherited the belief in demons as he inherited other beliefs, such as that gold and silver could corrupt; they were part of his Incarnation. There were various ways of casting them out, from spells to nauseous drinks. Skulls found with a hole in them suggest that in serious cases a skull might be trepanned to release a demon. "How do your pupils cast them out?" he asked
the Pharisees. He cast them out "by the finger of God". Lk 11.20
The demon who accompanied the man into the synagogue, a foolish thing to do, was alarmed by the sermon. Using
him as a ventriloquist uses his puppet, he cried out, "Have Mk 1.23f
you come to destroy us?" By "us" he meant the whole kingdom of demons. "We know you who you are, the holy one of God." Demons were the first Christians, recognizing him as the Son of God. "Stop speaking and come out of him", the Preacher commanded. Convulsing the man so that he uttered a loud cry, the demon departed.

When the minister closed the service with a prayer, eyes Mk 1.29f
which should have been looking up to heaven, were gazing at the wonder-working prophet. Some people followed him from the synagogue to find out where he lodged; then they went home and waited for the Sabbath to end. He did not so wait; encouraged by his first work of healing, he went to the upper room where his hostess lay ill with a fever, and, taking her by the hand, raised her to stand on her feet. Perhaps in her house he had lodged as a pupil at the synagogue school and so made the acquaintance of her son-in-law, Simon, and his brother Andrew; their immediate response to his call to be disciples suggests a familiar acquaintance. The hostess, sufficiently recovered, was providing a supper, when there came a loud knocking at the door. A horn-blast had announced the end of the Sabbath, and those who had followed him from the synagogue to his

lodging had come back, bringing sick friends to be his patients. Where there was no faith, as later at Nazareth, there were no cures. The healing of the demoniac even on the Sabbath, when the Pharisees forbade the practice of medicine, so inspired the patients that according to St Mark he healed them all.

Nervous cases were common in a country oppressed by
Rome, and he was much beset by patients. St Paul, who
heard of his work from his medical attendant, St Luke,
Acts 26.26 said, "These things were not done in a corner". But he
needed a corner if he was to be "alone, yet not alone", even
though it was only the corner of a field. Before his hostess
was awake he might slip away to a hillside behind the
town. Perhaps one morning at the sight of a sunrise he
said,

Mt 5.45 God maketh his sun to rise
on the evil and on the good.

He was near his Father in feeling that to both God was equally kind. He made a little poem of the idea, adding,

And he sendeth his rain
on the just and on the unjust.

He quoted it in the Sermon on the Mount, telling his
hearers that a sunrise or the autumn rain should be a
lesson to them to love their enemies. Even the simplest
things gave him a thought of God which was, in effect, the
sense of his presence. Poets had sung of famous gardens, as
the Garden of Alcinous, but in a wild flower, asphodel,
anemone, or gladiolus, he saw what gave the grass a richer
Mt 6.29 clothing than his royal robes gave Solomon. Poets had sung
of nightingales, almost as well as they sang themselves, but
he was attracted even by sparrows; not one fell to the
Mt 10.29 ground without God's knowledge. His Father loved and

enjoyed his world, and only at Creation had he rested for a day, the Sabbath; he did not rest on later Sabbaths. So he had not broken the Fourth Commandment, as the Pharisees would have alleged, by healing his hostess on the Sabbath.

But he could not confine himself to a corner, though as wide as a hillside; he was not in the world to be a monk like the Essenes of whom he had heard, practising a private religion by the Dead Sea. He was come to proclaim the Kingdom of God in the streets of Jerusalem; Mount Zion might be its headquarters. Meanwhile there was much ground to be covered, more than the hundred miles to Jerusalem. To limit his work, and yet to extend it, he needed disciples or, as the Aramaic word appears to mean, apprentices. Some of his followers were wondering if he would have a band of disciples like John the Baptist; it might raise for them a personal problem. In the *Fourth*
Gospel he says to Nathanael, "When thou wast under the Jn 1.48
figtree, I saw thee", a poetic way of saying he had read his private thoughts. A friend of Philip, he probably became the disciple called in the other Gospels Bartholemew. His Master was far from a figtree when he pondered over his
choice of disciples; he spent a night on a hillside in prayer. Lk 6.12

Probably with Simon and Andrew there was an understanding, but, poetic in his ways as in his words, he gave them a dramatic call. Fishermen, they were knee-deep in the Sea of Galilee with a castnet, when he beckoned to them
and cried, "Come, I will make you fishers of men". They Mt 4.19f
responded, as did two other fishermen, James and John, who were mending their net in a boat. Sailors with their experience of storms have often been God-fearing men; it may be significant that his first disciples were fishermen.

Mk 3.17 James and John, twins, he nicknamed Boanerges, Thunder-
bolts. Later, pretending to take the name seriously, they
Lk 9.54 asked if they might not call down fire from heaven on an
inhospitable Samaritan village; Elijah had destroyed men
with lightning; but he did not approve of the spirit in which
Mt 4.21f they spoke. That their father, Zebedee, had slaves fishing
Mt 27.55–6 in another boat, and that their mother, Salome, contri-
buted generously to the disciples' money-bag suggests they
Mt 9.9f left a profitable business. So also did Levi, the customs-
Lk 5.27f officer; perhaps the sacrifice gained him the nickname,
Matthew, Gift of God. A disciple who did not regard him
as a "gift of God" was Simon the Zealot; to him a customs-
officer was a publican, a traitor to his country. But no
doubt they became friends, the Nativity Canticle right in
saying, "He has come to guide our feet into the way of
Lk 1.79 peace". Of the other disciples the most promising appeared
to be Judas; the only one who was not a Galilean, he showed
a singular faith in becoming a disciple. He was given the
Jn 13.29 money-bag to carry, not an onerous task. Yet it became too
Mt 26.15 onerous when he added to it the thirty pieces of silver for
Mt 27.5 which he betrayed his Master, and he committed suicide.
There were twelve disciples in all. The number was
significant; as God had chosen the Twelve Tribes of Israel
to be his chosen people, so their Master had chosen twelve
disciples to be the founder of his Kingdom. In an unobtru-
sive way he played the same part as God.

Lk 11.1f "Lord, teach us to pray as John taught his disciples; the
answer was the Lord's Prayer. It might be more properly
called the Disciples' Prayer; he would not have joined with
Mt 6.9f them in saying "Our Father"; when he spoke to them of
God, it was either "your Father" or "my Father", never
"our Father". As there are two versions of it in the Gospels,

the disciples may not have repeated it as often as some later Christians. Yet in Aramaic it is a poem, with rhythm and not without rhyme, meant to be easily remembered. So also is a large part of the Sermon on the Mount. Perhaps it, too, is misnamed; the word translated "preach" means to be a herald. He was obviously a herald of the Good Time Coming in the remarkable couplet,

> Blessed are the meek, Mt 5.5
> for they shall inherit the earth.

Religion's natural language is poetic; the attempt to make statements about God in prose has been compared with the attempt to draw a map of the world on a flat surface. Almost all the prophets had spoken or written in verse. Isaiah wrote nothing, but his rhythmical sayings were easily remembered. Jeremiah taught for twenty years before he committed anything to writing. It was natural for this new Prophet, familiar with the old prophets, to speak often in a rhythmical style. Sometimes in saying something trivial he could not avoid a couplet:

> A disciple is not above his teacher, Mt 10.24
> nor a slave above his master;

still less could he avoid it in a momentous saying:

> Heaven and earth shall pass away, Mk 13.31
> but my words shall not pass away.

He was to need three lines for one of his greatest sayings,

> No man knoweth the Son save the Father, Lk 10.22
> and no man knoweth the Father save the Son,
> and he to whomsoever the Son shall reveal him,

a saying that speaks of his awesome sense of loneliness among men, and of much more.

Mt 7.13f He thought much in pictures, as "the strait gate", "the
Mt 15.14 narrow way", and "the blind leading the blind". "Let the
Mt 8.22 dead bury their dead" is a frightening picture. "Here is a
man on a bier bound hand and foot; and who are they that
are carrying him, those silent, awful figures, bound like
him hand and foot, moving swiftly and steadily with their
burden? It is the dead burying the dead." Some sayings are
whimsical; to Martha complaining that her sister sat
listening to him instead of helping to prepare the supper, he
Lk 10.42 said, "Mary has chosen the better dish". Yet at the same
time they could be serious; a charitable act was not to be
like a Temple service announced by a blast from a ram's
Mt 6.2 horn: "Do not blow a trumpet before you." At times he
could be sarcastic, even about his disciples. When Peter
Mk 10.28f pointed out that he and the others had left all to follow
him, he replied that no one who had left home or brothers
or sisters or father or mother or wife for his sake but would
receive an hundredfold, houses, brothers, sisters, mothers;
then, as though going too far, he quickly added "with
persecutions". He spoke sarcastically about Jerusalem:
Lk 13.33 "It cannot be that a prophet should perish outside Jerusalem." Yet he knew that many prophets from Isaiah to
John the Baptist had so perished. He must have been con-
scious that in a way he was God's one and only prophet. It
is not surprising that Peter misunderstood something he
Mt 17.27 said. When he pointed out that the Temple tax was due to
be paid, he was told to catch a fish and he would find the
half-shekel in its mouth. But Peter took no action, not
understanding that he was merely to catch and sell the
fish. Of course, it did not matter, the tax being one from
Mt 12.6 which he could feel himself exempt; as he said later, "One
is here greater than the Temple".

Of course, there were the parables; "without a parable Mk 4.34
spake he not unto them"; they made up about a third of his teaching. St Augustine interpreted the *Good Samaritan*: the man who fell among thieves was Adam, the thieves the Lk 10.30f
Devil and his angels; they stripped him, depriving him of his immortality, and left him half-naked, a poor sinful creature; the Good Samaritan who saved him was Christ, the inn to which he brought him the Church and the innkeeper the Apostle Paul. But the parables, apart from a few, are not allegories; they are stories in which the material order shows some affinity with the spiritual. Some may be stories of an actual happening, one, the *Unjust Steward*. But to emphasize a point a story could be Lk 16.1f
fantastic. In the *Unfaithful Servant* the man owed a fellow- Mt 18.23f
servant a hundred denarii, while to his master he owed a hundred million; our debt to our fellow-men is vastly less than our debt to God. *The Sower* has also a fantastic feature. Mk 4.3f
The smallholder sowed his seed in a patch of ground on the crumbling limestone rock. Some fell by the wayside, the thin path trod by villagers through the winter stubble; and some fell on stony ground, the soil thin over the rock, and some among thorns, the tall thistles that were the plague of Palestine. As ploughing came after sowing, seeds

that fell on the path were picked up by birds; of the plants produced by other seed, some were choked by a fresh crop of thistles and some were too shallow-rooted to grow. A tenfold return for the successful seed was considered a good harvest, but in the parable the return was preposterous, thirtyfold or sixtyfold or even a hundredfold. But he was thinking less of the smallholder than of himself sowing a different kind of seed. Much of it would be wasted, but the successful would have a heavenly return.

The Sower is so true to Palestinian conditions that one feels
it has a verbal authenticity. That is also true of the weather
forecasts: "When ye see a cloud from the west, ye say,
Lk 12.54 There cometh a shower; when ye see the south wind blow,
ye say, There will be heat"; Palestine had to the west the
Mediterranean Sea, the source of rain, and to the south the
hot arid desert. Only one who spoke Aramaic would have
Mt 6.26 said, "Behold the fowls of the air; they sow not nor reap,
Mt 6.28 nor carry into barns . . . Consider the lilies of the field, how
they grow; they toil not, neither do they spin"; in Aramaic,
Lk 12.24 birds, mostly called ravens, are masculine and flowers
feminine. Even when we have two versions of a saying, we
may tell the correct one by its more poetic quality. "If I
Lk 11.20 by the finger of God cast out demons" has been changed
Mt 12.28 by St Matthew into the less vivid, "If I by the Spirit of
God . . ."

Exorcisms were so common with medical practitioners
that they could hardly have failed to provide a parable. A
house stood on the edge of a desert, a dangerous position; a
demon, seeing it empty—of course the owner was at home,
being himself the house—empty of all grace of God,
entered and took possession. The owner, feeling its un-
Lk 11.24f comfortable presence, contrived to get rid of it, and had the
whole house swept and garnished. The demon must have
been a filthy housekeeper. Outcast, he wandered about the

dry places of the desert and gathered seven other demons, as bad as himself, or worse. They plotted together and one night came trooping to the house. They went about it, pushing their faces against the windows and, seeing no trace of the grace of God, entered and took possession. The owner was in a worse case than before. All exorcism of demons was not finally successful. "By whom do your Lk 11.19
pupils cast them out?" he asked the Pharisees. Perhaps it was by their own finger. He cast them out by the finger of God.

The Prodigal Son is remarkable, the most natural of the Lk 15.11f
parables yet an allegory. The younger son is the publicans and sinners, the elder brother the scribes and Pharisees; that the father is God is why there is no mention of mother. The father was asked by the younger brother to bestow on him the portion of goods he would be due to inherit. The request was not unusual; it enabled a young man to start his own business. The father granted it, giving him a third of his goods, the legal amount if he died intestate. But the younger brother's business was pleasure, and he departed into a far country. Probably it was Jerusalem, where in spite of the Holy Temple he could be far enough from his father. The elder brother ungraciously said he wasted his substance with harlots. Perhaps it was with bookmakers, for Herod the Great, a patron of the Olympic Games, had built in Jerusalem a large hippodrome as well as a theatre. To pay off his debts he sold the gold ring his father gave him when he had come of age. He may even have sold himself as a slave, for he was without shoes, which slaves were forbidden to wear. His work was feeding swine, a disgusting job for a Jew; he was glad to share their food, the hard husks of carob trees. But he remembered his father, who had never ceased remembering him. He had been keeping a constant outlook, for it was not by chance he

was on the flat housetop, where he saw the returning prodigal, while he was yet a great way off. And he was moved by compassion. As the father is God, this is an extraordinary revelation of his attitude to sinners. And the story goes on: "He ran and fell on his neck and kissed him." He called for another ring for his finger and shoes for his feet. He even called for the killing of the fatted calf. "There is joy among the angels over one sinner that repenteth." Had the self-righteous uncharitable elder brother repented, there would have been joy among the archangels.

Lk 11.20 "If I by the finger of God cast out demons, then is the
Kingdom of God come upon you." That the people ex-
pected; that times were bad made its immediate coming
more likely; it had to be preceded by the "Messianic
Woes". John, beheaded by Herod, had proved a disappoint-
ment, and people thronged to this new prophet. Twice St
Mk 3.20 Mark speaks of the food situation: "the multitudes coming
Mk 6.31 together, they could not so much as eat bread"; "they had
Lk 12.1 no leisure to eat". "An innumerable multitude" and "they
trod one upon another", says St Luke. St Peter told him the
Lk 5.3 Lord had asked him to launch his boat on the Lake. Its
seat was not an awkward pulpit, for he did not stand on it;
like the Greek orators he sat when he spoke. "And he sat
down" is often the prelude to a discourse in the Gospels.
And "looked" and "said" often go together; the look was
part of the proclamation. And how strangely he spoke of
Mt 5.21f himself. "Thus saith the Lord" Isaiah and Jeremiah had
begun, but he began "I say unto you". He even contra-
dicted the Law, read by God himself on the Sabbath;
"Ye have heard it said of old time, but I say unto you".
Mk 1.27 St Mark describes the people's amazement: "What is this?"
Mk 6.2 "A new teaching?" "Whence hath this man these things".

Some said he was Elijah who, caught up to heaven, had returned to earth; others said he was Jeremiah who, the Temple destroyed, buried the Ark of the Covenant on Mount Nebo and would restore it when the Messiah was about to appear. The secret of himself he would keep till he could proclaim it at the right time and in the right place, in a sermon in the synagogue of Nazareth. Mt 16.14

The Pharisees, the Separate Ones, did not stand aloof from this new Prophet; they approved of his proclamation of the Coming Kingdom; it was to hasten it that they were the Separate Ones, pietists. They even kept the whole of the Fourth Commandment; though it is mainly about the observance of the Sabbath, it begins, "Six days shalt thou labour"; the great Hillel himself followed a trade. The scribes, many of them Pharisees, would listen intently to what the Prophet taught; they were so concerned about the scrupulous keeping of the Law that they planted about it the Mishnah, the Hedge, supplementary rules and regulations to render impossible any unconscious breach of the Law. Some Pharisees, far from unfriendly, invited him to their house to share a meal, an intimate communion. No doubt it was to enquire about the Coming Kingdom. Lk 7.36f

But he was not always as well entertained. It was reported he had feasted with the customs-house officer in Capernaum, Levi, other publicans present; he had been the boon companion of publicans and sinners, for publicans were sinners, working on the Sabbath. Many Pharisees became suspicious of this new Prophet. What was his own attitude to the Law? To eat with unwashen hands did not defile a man, he was reported to have said. Yet it needed only a few drops of water to save the hands from ceremonial uncleanness, and the matter was so important that Lk 5.27f Mt 15.20

the Essene monks took a bath before a meal. Then there
Mt 15.17f was his saying that what defiled a man was not what went
into him, but what came out; yet all he meant was that to
swallow down pork was not as bad as to spew up unkind
words. And were his disciples careful as to what they ate,
meat always kosher, prepared according to the Law, and
never unclean meat, as pig, hare, or rabbit? Perhaps they
were; the Apostle Peter had never eaten anything common
Acts 10.14 or unclean. But he said that some Pharisees did worse than
swallow down a pig; they strained at a gnat and swallowed
Mt 23.24 a camel. Scrupulous as to their own actions, they passed
very uncharitable judgements on the lives of other people.

Even more questionable was the disciples' keeping of the
Sabbath. It was the only day in the week with a name; the
others had numbers. Gathered on the Sabbath, manna in
Ex 16.20 the wilderness bred worms and stank; the Children of
Israel had to gather a double portion the day before. By the
scribes and Pharisees the day was kept so strictly that
whether or not it was lawful to eat an egg laid on the
Sabbath was debated; there were two schools of thought.
Mk 2.23f Yet a smallholder reported that the disciples had picked
and eaten corn on the Sabbath. The Law allowed a man to
eat another man's corn so long as he did not cut it with a
sickle; he could even enter a vineyard and eat grapes; "But
Deut 23.24 thou shalt not put any in thy vessel". Tacitus remarked on
the way Jews shared things with their fellow-countrymen.
Of course, the smallholder may have disliked the sight of
twelve men in his cornfield, but the only accusation he
could make was that they had rubbed the ears of corn
between their hands, a form of threshing, a labour forbidden on the Sabbath. The Pharisees to whom he reported
the matter agreed with the accusation; the Sabbath was

made for feasting, not for threshing. But he defended the
disciples: "The Sabbath was made for man, and not man Mk 2.27
for the Sabbath", a fantastic interpretation of the Fourth
Commandment.

But the Pharisees had yet another complaint: his dis- Mk 2.18
ciples did not fast like the disciples of John the Baptist, or
like their own pupils, taught to fast as they did themselves
on two days of the week, Monday and Thursday. He did not
disapprove of fasting; in the wilderness he had fasted like
the Baptist on locusts and honey gathered from bushes;
what he disapproved of was people putting on faces when
they fasted, even sprinkling their hair with dust and ashes.

> But when you fast, Mt 6.17
> anoint your head and wash your face,

he said to his disciples with a humorous smile. They were
to treat a fast as though it were a festival. And he excused
them from fasting in the circumstances; "Can the children Mk 2.19
of the bridechamber fast while the bridegroom is with
them?" It was a bold thing to say, expressing a sense of unity
with God, for in *Isaiah* God is the bridegroom of his people:
"As the bridegroom rejoiceth over his bride, so thy God Isa 62.5
rejoiceth over thee." But, at least, it was a poetic descrip-
tion of the joyful fellowship between himself and his
disciples. They were like the wedding guests who, so far Judg 14.10,15
from fasting, feasted for a week at Samson's wedding, and Tobit 8.19
at Tobias's for a fortnight. But the time would come when
he would be taken from them and then they would fast.
Something had begun to occupy his mind that was far from
a wedding: a funeral.

The Baptist had called on people to repent; he told them,
even publicans and sinners, that their righteousness must Mt 5.20
exceed the righteousness of the scribes and Pharisees. But
they were held in high respect; bound to their religion by a

strict obedience, they prayed, fasted, gave alms, and
studied Holy Scripture. Yet it was one who was himself a
Rom 10.2 Pharisee, St Paul, who said that while they had a zeal for
God it was not according to knowledge. There was a
knowledge of God truer and more intimate than the Law
and the Prophets could impart. It was imparted by him
Mt 11.28 who said, "Come unto me", as though he were God's
intermediary. One more than a prophet, one in a unique
Mt 11.9 relationship to God. Yet God was so transcendent that men
could not pray to him directly; "I am Raphael one of the
Tobit 12.14 seven holy angels, who present the prayers of the faithful",
said the archangel to Tobit. Pharisees in Jerusalem sent
scribes to Galilee to bring back a report of this prophet;
perhaps the worst they reported was that he appeared to
have no sense of sin.

Lk 13.31f Some Galilean Pharisees seemed friendly; they advised
him to leave Galilee, his life in danger from the tetrarch
Herod. "Go and tell that fox", he began. Herod was a fox;
he had sent them himself; he wanted him out of the tetrarchy, envious of his popularity, but too afraid of it to
put him to death. "I cast out demons and heal diseases
today and tomorrow and on the third day I complete my
task"; the words express the fullness and roundness of his
allotted span. "Nevertheless I must journey on, today,
tomorrow and the next day; it cannot be that a prophet
perish out of Jerusalem." In any case Galilee could no
longer be his headquarters; in Capernaum his popularity
was too facile, while on the other hand "Woe unto thee,
Lk 10.13 Chorazin" and "Woe unto thee, Bethsaida", he said of two
neighbouring towns.

Mk 4.35f His first departure from Galilee was to the other side of the
Lake, Decapolis. He hoped to find there a restful peace,

but he found it even in the boat, though it was being tossed up and down in a storm. Taking no part in the rowing, perhaps because he was unable to row, he had fallen asleep. The storm was one of the evening squalls caused by a great wind sweeping down the Jordan Valley from the heights of Hermon. The alarmed disciples woke him with some wild hope he would still the storm. But these evening squalls soon subside, and he awoke only to play the part of a dramatic poet, rebuking the wind and saying to the sea, "Peace, be still". But he may have quieted the disciples, quoting as though prophetic of himself the words of a psalm,

> He maketh the storm a calm, Ps. 107.29
> so that the waves thereof are still.

The time was short, and journeying with his disciples Mk 6.7f
he could not cover much ground. So he sent them two by two on a mission to proclaim the Kingdom. He gave them power to cast out demons and to cure diseases, not a
miraculous power. Roads were hilly and rough, and if he Mt 10.5f
told them to take neither staff nor sandals it was his figurative way of saying that their mission was as sacred as a visit to the Holy Temple, when staff and sandals were left behind. They were to avoid a thoroughfare leading to Samaria or the Gentile world; their mission was to the lost sheep of the House of Israel, the lapsed masses for whom the religious leaders felt no responsibility. They
would not always be welcomed, but "Peace be to this Lk 10.6
house", they were to say; and "if a son of peace is not there", the greeting not well received, "your peace will come back to you", it will bless the heart that offered it. He himself
went further afield, perhaps unwillingly following his Mk 7.24f
widening reputation as a healer, as far as the border of Tyre and Sidon. There a woman asked him to drive a

demon out of her little daughter. The Jews had a saying, "It is not meet to take the children's bread and give it to the dogs". Gentiles were dogs because they were enemies of God. He misquoted the saying with "give it to the little dogs". She appreciated his promising humour and said, "O yes, sir, but the little dogs under the table get the children's crumbs".

Mk 3.22 His reputation for casting out demons was so great that the Pharisees felt they had to offer an explanation: he cast them out by Beelzebub, the prince of demons. "Lord of flies", those carriers of infectious diseases, Beelzebub had been propitiated by the Philistines; now in Palestine, named after them, he was more highly honoured by being given the title, Prince of Demons. That the Pharisees said he cast out demons by Beelzebub is convincing evidence of his almost miraculous gift of healing. It was also in a way a high personal tribute that he was possessed, not by one demon or like Mary Magdalene by seven, but by the prince of demons himself. But when the Pharisees' explanation was reported to him, he said their sin was unpardonable,
Mk 3.28f being a sin against the Holy Ghost. Already he was anticipating the article in the Christian Creed, "incarnate by the Holy Ghost".

"Widow" occurs so often in the Gospels, he must have had
Lk 2.36 an unusual feeling for widows as he had for children. That Anna, daughter of Phanuel, gave thanks for the Child in the Temple seems appropriate; she had been a widow for about seventy-seven years. What inspired his feeling for widows was partly a thoughtful love for his mother, Mary.
Lk 4.16f So with his mind, if not his eyes, turned to fateful Jerusalem, he paid what would probably be his last visit to Nazareth. And it seemed the most suitable place to proclaim himself

more than a prophet. As a rabbi he was invited to preach in the synagogue on the Sabbath morning. The service began as always with the Shema, "Hear, O Israel, the Lord our God is one Lord". No doubt he bowed his head, yet, more than a prophet, he may have wondered if God was so total a unity. The Elder continued the service by reading the Law, as prescribed by the lectionary, each verse read in Hebrew and followed by a translation in Aramaic. Then the Deacon took from the Ark the roll of the Prophets and, removing the linen cover, handed it to the rabbi who was to preach. He opened the roll—it almost opened itself—at *Isaiah*, at a passage where a prophet of the Exile speaks of
the Lord's Anointed. He began to read: "The Spirit of the Isa 61
Lord God is upon me; because he hath anointed me to preach good tidings to the meek, to bind up the broken-hearted...." Suddenly he stopped in the middle of the sentence. John the Baptist would have gone on reading, "and to proclaim the day of vengeance of our God". John had proclaimed that the Lord's Anointed would baptize with fire. But that was not his message or his mission. Omitting the words he went on to read, "to give beauty for ashes, the oil of joy for mourning, the garment of praise for the spirit of heaviness". The Lesson ended, he closed the roll and handing it back to the Deacon sat down to preach. "This day is the Scripture fulfilled in your ears." If their ears were open to hear the good news of the Coming Kingdom, their eyes were wider open to look with wonder on this strange preacher who claimed to be, not a prophet, but the One of whom the prophets had spoken. There was no payment to a rabbi for preaching, but if there had been he would not have received it. Elders sitting behind him became restless; then one of them springing to his feet cried, "Is not this the carpenter's son?" There was an uproar; men rose from the stone seat along the wall or from

their mats on the floor, while women, one of them Mary, shrank behind their barrier. "All the congregation were filled with rage." Shouting "Blasphemy", they bustled him out of the building towards a hill-ridge from which he could be thrown down and, the punishment for blasphemy, stoned to death. But his sudden awe-inspiring appearance saved him; "Passing through the midst of them, he went his way". He had preached his last sermon in a synagogue. The experience helped him to decide on his next step, the hundred miles' walk to Jerusalem. If a prophet could not perish outside the sacred city, still less could one who was more than a prophet.

Mt 11.19 "Son of man" he began to call himself: "the Son of Man
came eating and drinking"; it was to become his almost
Lk 9.22 invariable name for himself: "the Son of Man must suffer
many things". Yet he is not so called by anyone else in the
Acts 7.56 New Testament except by the visionary martyr, Stephen.
The name was ambiguous. It might be a poetical synonym for man, suggesting that man was a creaturely being compared with God's holy angels:

Ps 8.4 What is man that thou art mindful of him,
or the son of man that thou visitest him?

Dan 7.13, 18f But in the *Book of Daniel* it had become a high title, given
not to an individual but to a divinely appointed people, "Saints of the Most High". They contrasted with bestial heathen peoples, such as the Babylonians, a lion with an eagle's wings, or the Assyrians, a bear with three ribs in its mouth, or with the Persians, a leopard with four wings of a fowl and four heads. But in the *Book of Enoch* the idea was narrowed down to a heavenly pre-existent Being, waiting at God's throne to represent him at the coming Judgement

and preside over a purified theocracy. Sometimes he was called the Messiah, the Anointed. So Son of Man was ambiguous perhaps chosen for its ambiguity. When he said, "The Son of Man hath not where to lay his head", Mt 8.20
he might mean that as a wandering rabbi he could not be sure of the hospitality enjoyed by some rabbis, who devoured widows' houses. Or it might be a poetical way of describing his awesome sense of loneliness among men, which even his disciples could not share or relieve. The ambiguity was a safeguard; he could not be accused of making a high claim which, most Pharisees unfriendly and Herod watchful, might have brought about his immediate end. As things were, Mary and his brothers were anxious; Mk 3.31
they tried to force their way into a crowded meeting to take him home; they alleged he was not in his right mind. Mk 3.21
Nor was he, unless he was Son of Man in both senses, human and divine.

His popularity facile, the leaders of religion unfriendly,
his own family not sympathetic, he was beginning to feel
that his life's work was death; from fateful Jerusalem he
would not return to Galilee. So he decided to give a farewell
feast to his Galilean followers. To them it would be a fore-
taste of the Heavenly Banquet. That was mainly based on
Isa 25.6 Isaiah's words about the Lord making for his people a feast
of fat things, of fat things full of marrow, of wine on the lees
well refined. To the few rich people, who fared sumptu-
ously every day, the picture might not greatly appeal;
but most people were poor, partaking of meat only on the
Ps 104.26 Sabbath, and with them the picture was popular, leviathan
Job 40.15 providing the fish and behemoth the meat, while wine
cups were frequently refilled. But the Son of Man greatly
Lk 14.15 modified the idea; "Blessed is he that shall eat bread in the
Kingdom of God". Also he included among the guests
Mt 8.11 other than Jews; "Many shall come from the east and from
the west and shall recline with Abraham, Isaac and Jacob in
the Kingdom of Heaven". The picture occurs in the parable
Lk 16.19f *The Rich Man and Lazarus*, and there it is less of feasting
than of heavenly fellowship, Lazarus reclining on Abraham's bosom. Of course, the picture would not have been
satisfactory to the self-righteous without its opposite, the

picture of Gehenna or Hell-fire. It, too, grew out of words
of Isaiah; they are about transgressors: "Their worm shall Isa 66.24
not die, neither shall their fire be quenched." The picture
was continually before the eyes of the people of Jerusalem,
for Gehenna was the Valley of Hinnom, lying south-west
of the city. Polluted by human sacrifices to Moloch in the 2 Kings 16.2f
time of Ahaz, it was a suitable place for the city's refuse, Mk 9.43–4
left to decay slowly, the worm dying not, or burnt, the
fire not quenched, smoke still rising. The picture is elabor-
ately described in *The Book of Enoch*, and to some Pharisees
was familiar. As the incarnate Son of Man he inherited the
picture and used it for its graphic value. Though he spoke
of eternal punishment, by eternal he did not mean lasting
for ever; he meant characteristic of the Age to come. God
would not condemn to everlasting punishment those he so
cared for that, as he said to them, "the very hairs of your Lk 12.7
head are all numbered". That he believed in bodies being
burned in Hell is no more likely than that he believed
that the leviathan and behemoth were cooked in Heaven.

The farewell feast he gave his Galilean followers was not Mk 6.30f
in their own country, but on the other side of the Lake; his
acts could be symbolic like his words. Someone retained a
clear memory of the scene, the grass green on the hillside. Mk 6.39
It was late spring or early summer; in less than a year he
would give another farewell feast, not on a hillside, but in
an upper chamber in Jerusalem. That the guests reclined
on the grass in regular groups suggests ritual. And the
feast had ceremonial acts much the same as the Last
Supper: he took bread—he blessed it—he gave thanks—he Mk 6.41
gave it to them. In the *Fourth Gospel* the story takes the Jn 6.1f
place of the Last Supper and is followed by a discourse on Jn 6.26f
the Eucharist. That the guests did not understand its
sacramental significance, yet felt its importance, suggests
how it grew into a fantastic story, the feeding of five

thousand on a few loaves and fishes. That would not seem
2 Kings 4.1f impossible; Elisha had performed the same kind of miracle
though on a smaller scale. But for him the miracle was
impossible; it would have been a yielding to the first
temptation in the wilderness, figuratively described as the
changing of stones into bread. Even the disciples did
not fully understand the significance, for he sent them
away in the boat to return to Capernaum, while he re-
Jn 6.15f mained on the hillside. It was part of his "awesome sense
of loneliness" that he could not pray with his disciples.
Also on this occasion it was mainly for them he prayed.
Jn 6.19 That was why, rowing their boat on the Lake, they saw
him walking on the water; he was projected to them as an
apparition.

With the disciples he left Galilee and travelled into the
north country; there he would be free from the police of
Herod Antipas, not in danger of being put to death outside
Jerusalem, the holy city. But his main desire was to have
freedom to talk with his disciples and put to them a
Mt 16.13f question. He waited to put it till, still travelling northward,
they came in sight of Caesarea Philippi, named after the emperor who had built it and after the tetrarch who had enlarged it, Philip's City of Caesar. Birthplace of the river Jordan and of the Greek god Pan, both born in a cave haunted by nymphs, it had an ancient fame. But Philip's father, Herod the Great, had exalted it to heaven by building a temple to Caesar Augustus; it was in memory of his visit, as was also his divine statue, set hard by the shrine of Pan. Resplendent with white marble, the temple stood on the summit of a rocky ridge. Pointing to it, the symbol of imperial Rome, he put to his disciples the question, "Whom do ye say that I am?" They were perturbed; they believed he was more than a prophet, but was he the Christ, the Anointed? For him Pharisees and zealots were waiting,

though with different views, and pious men like Simeon,
"looking for the consolation of Israel", and even pious Lk 2.25
women like Anna, "looking for the redemption of Jeru- Lk 2.38
salem". God reigned over all, but Satan and his angels had
taken possession of the lower heavens and were working
great evil, especially through Rome. God now appeared too
exalted to take further part in human history, but he
would act through the medium of the Messiah, the Christ.
But their Master did not look to the disciples like God's
exalted king. Perhaps Peter remembered the success
of the demonic mission on which he had sent them,
greeting them on their return, "I beheld Satan as lightning Lk 10.18
fallen from heaven", and "Thou art the Christ", he cried. Mt 16.16
"Blessed art thou, Simon, flesh and blood hath not revealed
it to thee, but my Father in heaven." That had been his own
case: at his Baptism a voice from heaven had said, almost
audibly, "Thou art my beloved Son". Mk 1.11

In one of his genealogical tables he has the surname Mt 1.1
Christ, as also he had for St Paul, "our Lord Jesus Christ".
It became so common that one almost imagines that Jesus
was his Christian name. Yet it was only a title, the Anointed.
He never claimed it; when John in prison sent two of his
disciples to ask if he was the Christ, he gave them the
cryptic answer, "Blessed is he whosoever shall not be Mt 11.6
offended in me". Yet he never disclaimed it; when they
were gone, he told his own disciples that John was Elijah Mt 11.14
the Messiah's forerunner. But he straitly charged his Mt 16.20
disciples not to speak of him as the Christ. He was so far
from being that triumphant figure people expected that he
felt that, Son of Man, he must suffer many things and be Mt 16.21f
put to death. The disciples were aghast about what he foretold them of himself; "Far be it from thee, Lord", Peter
cried. His reply to Peter seems harsh, "Get thee behind me,
Satan". But it was not to his faithful friend he was speaking;

Lk 4.8 he was quoting what he had said in the wilderness to Satan,
who had returned and was tempting him through Peter to
play the part of an insurrectionist or revolutionary politician. Son of Man, he was humbler than the regal Christ
people expected, yet in his own mind he was more exalted.
He might have applied to himself the closing words of the
Lk 3.38 geneaological table, "Son of Adam, Son of God". He was
the first to believe in the Christian doctrine of the Incarnation.

What he said of the suffering Son of Man had alarmed the
disciples; some were wondering why they had become
disciples. Would not his Heavenly Father communicate
with them in some reassuring way? He waited a week;
Mt 17.1f then, choosing three disciples, Peter, James, and John, an
inner circle—all twelve would have been too many, a
distracting number—he took them on a mountain expedi-
tion. Men felt nearer God on a mountain; the Lord gave
Ex 31.18 the Law to Moses on Mount Sinai and to Elijah a revelation
1 Kings 19.8f on Mount Horeb. The mighty Hermon with its snow-
capped summit had been dear to him since the early days
when he viewed it from the hilltop behind Nazareth. The
ascent was easy, but laborious for fishermen after a walk of
more than ten miles, and they were still far from the summit when they lay down in the shelter of a wood of small
trees. Clouds gather through the night on Hermon and
descend white and cold as though they were half-melted
snow. Chilled Peter awoke early in the morning. He saw
what made him rouse his drowsy companions, their Master
kneeling in prayer, so rapt a look on his face that they felt
they were beholding a vision. "He was transfigured before
them." To so heavenly a figure the morning mist seemed a
suitable garment, "shining, exceeding white as snow".

Peter remembered that before they settled down to sleep he had discoursed to them about Moses and Elijah, explaining that his mission was in harmony with the Law and the Prophets; "and, behold, there appeared unto them Moses and Elijah talking with him". So Peter told the evangelist St Mark, perhaps believing what he said, or inspired to speak in his Master's highly symbolic style. He even longed for the vision to last. Remembering the joyous Jewish festival, the Feast of Booths, so named because all healthy adults slept in booths made of branches of living trees Peter pointed to the wood and cried, "Let us make three booths, one for thee, one for Moses and one for Elijah". "But he knew not what he said." One greater than Moses and Elijah was speaking from the overshadowing cloud, the Shekinah, from which, an indication of his presence, yet a concealment of his glory, God had spoken to the patriarchs; "This is my beloved Son, hear him", said the Voice. Peter had taken literally what his Master told the disciples of the Voice that spoke to him at his baptism. The same Voice was again so speaking to that kneeling rapt figure that Peter felt he was overhearing it himself. Whatever the experience of the Transfiguration amounted to factually, it meant a climax in his Master's mission. The writer of the Fourth Gospel does not report the story; there was no need; he could say, "We beheld his glory, the Jn 1.14
glory as of the only begotten of the Father, full of grace and truth".

Coming away from the mountain, he came back to Mt 17.14f
earth. He was met by an excited crowd with a man shouting "Master"; His disciples had failed to heal his demoniac boy. He almost reproached them for their insufficient faith. His experience on the mountain had made him gravely anxious about interference with his mission; acts of healing must no longer mislead people as to its true nature.

But he healed the boy, the last work of its kind in Galilee.

His immediate mission was to proclaim the Kingdom; St Luke, a Gentile, calls it the Kingdom of God, St Mark and St Matthew, Jews, reverencing the Divine Name, call it the Kingdom of Heaven. There were varying views of its nature, but the disciples should have known what it essentially meant for their Master, the first petition of his Prayer being

Mt 6.10 Thy kingdom come,
thy will be done,
on earth as in heaven.

God's Kingdom was his rule over men's lives. "Except ye
Mt 18.3 become as little children", united to God as they are to
their parents, "ye shall not enter the kingdom ofheaven."
Their entrance might be a sudden conversion; it would be
Mt 13.44 like a rich treasure, buried in a time of invasion, ploughed
up by a smallholder; or it might come after a long seeking
Mt 13.45f and sacrifice; then it would be like a precious pearl, more
glamorous than Cleopatra's famous pearl, that a merchant
had long sought and sold all his possessions to purchase.

The Beatitudes are a poem about its blessedness.

Mt 5.3 Blessed are the poor in spirit,—
those who feel undeserving—
for theirs is the kingdom of heaven.

Mt 11.11 There had not been a greater born of woman than John
the Baptist, but he that was least in the Kingdom of Heaven
was greater than he.

If anyone sue thee for thy shirt, Mt 5.40
let him have thy cloak as well—

leaving you naked—;

If anyone strikes you on your right cheek, Mt 5.39
turn to him the other also—

let the insulting slap with the back of his hand be followed with the full weight of his fist on your face. Such couplets with their paradoxical sharpness were his way of saying, "Take no revenge; debts and insults are of small account compared with the blessedness of the Kingdom of Heaven."
That was also true of the greatest prosperity; "What shall Mk 8.36
it profit a man, if he gain the whole world and lose his own soul?" Life has no meaning apart from a divine destiny in the Kingdom of Heaven.

But the invocation "Our Father" should have told the disciples that for them in some small measure the Kingdom was already come; "Thy kingdom come" is a petition that it may spread. God was the Father of Israel; he told Moses
to say to Pharaoh, "Israel is my son, even my firstborn". Ex 4.22
Or he might be the Father of Israel's king; "This day have I Ps 2.7
begotten thee", he says in the Coronation Psalm. But no psalmist addressed God as Father, nor was he so addressed
in the Judaism of the disciples' time. Yet apart from the Mk 15.34
cry on the cross God for him was always Father; and while he would not have repeated with his disciples the Lord's Prayer, he gave them a share of his sense of Sonhood. So to that extent for them the Kingdom had come. And there was himself; though ultimately the Kingdom was beyond time and space, eternal life he sometimes called it, it had come into history in the person of their Master, so that he could say,

Lk 10.24 Many prophets and kings have desired to see
those things which ye see
and have not seen them;
And to hear those things which ye hear
and have not heard them.

Yet all was but small beginnings. Even "the Messianic Woes", the catastrophe people expected before the Kingdom, might have suggested the fateful part he had to play in its coming. But if he quoted the Second Isaiah about the
Isa 53.3f Suffering Servant, "a man of sorrows, wounded for our transgressions, bruised for our iniquities", he also saw himself as the Son of Man pictured by the prophet Daniel:
Mt 25.31 "The son of man shall come in glory and all his holy angels with him." He knew his death would be a crucifixion, yet at the same time a coronation.

The disciples were far from reassured; "And they were in
Mk 10.32 the way going to Jerusalem; and Jesus went before them, and they were amazed; and as they followed, they were afraid". But he thought of others who might be afraid. Though his family had protested he was not in his right mind, he expressed a warm religious unity with them
Mt 12.50 when he said, "Whosoever doeth the will of my Father, the same is my brother, and sister, and mother". As the family might be alarmed by his journey to Jerusalem, he paid a final visit to Nazareth, leaving his disciples at Capernaum. Whatever he told his mother, she decided to make the journey herself for the coming Passover. It was a long unusual journey for a widow. She remembered that she had made it about eighteen years before with Joseph; that had been for her Son's confirmation; this time, though she did not know it, it would be for his baptism. "I have a

baptism to be baptized withal, and how am I straitened Lk 12.50
till it be accomplished."

At Jericho was Elisha's Well; its bitter water the prophet 2 Kings 2.19f
had healed with a cruse of salt, creating in the stony Judean wilderness an oasis of palm-trees, balsam-groves, and roses; it might have inspired the disciples with fresh faith in their —they could not call him a prophet; he had said the last prophet was John the Baptist, implying he was more. They might also have been encouraged by the crowd that came from the city's narrow streets to hail him in the open, to them a Galilean prophet and wonder-worker. One man
climbed a sycamore tree by the roadside to view him over Lk 19.1f
people's heads. If he was small in stature, he was not a small man officially, being the chief custom officer on an important caravan route, employing clerks. He had left the custom-house to view the prophet, reported to be friendly with those the Pharisees called "publicans and sinners". Pointing to him a disciple said in a whisper, "Zacchaeus". He was one of two disciples that according to his custom he had sent into the city to enquire about hospitality, and had received their report. Looking up at him in the tree, he said, "Zacchaeus, make haste and come down, for today I will abide in thy house". Zacchaeus made haste. His pious parents had called him Zacchaeus, hoping he would live up to the name, which means pure. He was pure at least of what the Pharisees accused him of, the love of money that made him a custom officer and a traitor to his country. Perhaps he felt it wise to explain how free he was from such an offence; "Half my goods I give to the poor", he said. But treated by the Pharisees as the worst publican and sinner in Jericho, he had given up the practice of religion. "This day is salvation come to thy house", said the Galilean prophet. Next day, the Sabbath, he did not break the Fourth Commandment by working in the

custom house; he went with his family to morning service in the synagogue.

Perhaps the Galilean Prophet was the one who broke the
Fourth Commandment, walking more than the two
thousand cubits allowed by the Law on the Sabbath.
Certainly he was not invited to preach in the synagogue,
lodging in the house of Zacchaeus. Within a week of his
death, as he forecast it, he may have longed to be "alone,
Jn 16.32 yet not alone", and leaving the disciples in Jericho he may
have wandered into the wilderness. He may even have
visited the scene of his Baptism by the River Jordan, and
heard, clearer than an echo, the Divine Voice, "Thou art
my beloved Son". The scribes, subtle lawyers, could find
excuses for walking more than the two thousand cubits on
the Sabbath; for him there was no excuse; he could only
Lk 6.5 feel that, as he said, "the Son of Man is Lord of the Sabbath".
That, of course, was very near saying that God, his Heavenly
Father, and he were one.

Leaving Jericho early next morning, the Sunday, he and
his disciples were joined by other pilgrims to Jerusalem
for the Passover. Many of them would not walk the seven-
teen hilly miles, but, waiting for their caravan, they saw the
Prophet on his way. Outside the city, clad in a cloak of the
Mk 10.46f chill spring morning, sat by the wayside a blind beggar,
well-known in Jericho, Bartimaeus. Told who was passing
by, "Jesus, Son of David", he cried giving him an honorific
title, "have mercy on me". Healing according to the
prophets was a sign of the New Age:

Isa 35.6 Then shall the lame man leap as an hart,
and the tongue of the dumb shall sing;

but he was not the herald of the New Age people expected,

an exalted Israel or a heavenly Aeon. Works of healing might mislead them into thinking he was; there was a conflict between the sense of his mission and the kindness of his heart. He had solved the conflict at Bethsaida, when
he took a blind man out of the town that there would be Mk 8.22f
no witnesses of what people might imagine was a sign of their Kingdom. "Jesus, Son of David, have mercy on me", Bartimaeus kept calling. He stood still and silent; then he commanded him to be called. That Bartimaeus, flinging off his cloak, was able to find his way suggests that he had not been born blind. And he did not need to have spittle put on his eyes like the blind man of Bethsaida, or the blind man who, as Tacitus and Suetonius relate, was healed in that way by the Emperor Vespasian. But to the spectators the healing was one of the mighty acts of which they had heard. As there had been few such cases since he left Galilee, it raised high hopes in the disciples that he would perform others in Jerusalem, confirming his claim that the Kingdom had come. That the other pilgrims were impressed helped to pave the way for his triumphal entry into the Holy City.

The city was thronged with pilgrims, who had left their tents or sleeping-bags on the Mount of Olives. The Jews were a dispersed people, and for a festival like the Passover they came from as far east as Babylon and as far west as Rome, "many thousands of people from many thousands of towns", says Philo. Some were expecting the Galilean prophet, herald of the Messiah, if not the Messiah himself. The story of the healing of the blind beggar at Jericho
spread the interest and heightened the expectation. His Mt 21.1f
entry was greeted with the waving of palm-branches as had been the triumphal entry of Judas Maccabaeus; but to

many he appeared to be greater than that national hero. Riding into the city on an ass, he was expounding a text from the prophet Zechariah, himself the exposition: "Re-
Zech 9.9 joice greatly, O daughter of Zion; behold thy king cometh unto thee, lowly and riding upon an ass." The Galilean pilgrims at least, warm-hearted men, proudly welcomed him riding into a city where Galileans were despised, even for their northern accent. They hailed him as the Messiah, shouting "Hosanna, save now". For years they and others had been waiting for the Messiah who would establish the Kingdom of which Isaiah prophesied, "In the last days the mountain of the Lord's house shall be established on
Isa 2.2 the top of the mountain [Mount Zion?] and exalted above the hills". A Passover was the time he would come; at the Paschal Supper people left a door open, even food on the table, for his forerunner, Elijah. At last he had come as Zechariah foretold, "lowly and riding upon an ass". "Hosanna, save now" they kept shouting. When some Pharisees protested, he pointed to the great stones of the
Lk 19.39f Temple: "If these were silent, the very stones would cry out." "Sermons in stones", no doubt; yet the basic stones of the Temple under their heavy weight had a dejected look and might not have cried out. His triumphal entry into the holy City was a failure. Though he presented the picture of the Coming One as the prophet foretold, he was not what people expected, a Davidic king, or at least a revolutionary leader. A Palestinian ass, a large creature, could hold up its head as high as a horse but, not used in war like a horse, it was a symbol of peace, in his case peace with imperial Rome. Some disciples, waving palm-branches, may have hopefully shouted, "Hosanna, save now"; Judas, a deep thinker, felt this Messiah was a sham.

His attitude to women, like his attitude to children, was
very uncommon for his time, even unique. According to
the *Book of Enoch* God created no wives for his angels; they
were not worth creating. The Law allowed a man to divorce
his wife for almost any reason; the woman of Samaria to
whom he said in the Fourth Gospel, "Thou hast had five Jn 4.18
husbands", may have been merely a bad cook. But a
woman could not divorce a husband, her superior. He
rejected the Law; the man had no such superiority. So
women figure frequently in the Gospels, especially in St
Luke's Gospel. Compared with Xenophon's *Memorabilia*
that Gospel reads like a novel; it even tells us the name of
the wife of Herod's chancellor, Joanna. Suitably a woman Lk 8.3
comes into his first evening in Jerusalem. So do children on Mk 11.11
the following morning, shouting "Hosanna". The angry Mt 21.15–16
scribes and high priests asked if he did not know what they Ps. 8.2
were shouting. He replied by quoting a psalm, "Out of the
mouth of babes and sucklings thou hast brought praise to
perfection". It was no wonder he took children in his
arms.

As the woman is often mistaken for a harlot who also
interrupted a meal with an alabaster flask of ointment, she Mk 14.3f
might be given a name; living in Bethany she could be
called the Lady of the House of Dates. Though more than
a mile from Jerusalem, the village was considered part of
the sacred city. There lived a man, Simon the Leper. But
lepers were not allowed to live among other people;
"Uzziah lived in a several house, being a leper"; but Simon 2 Chr 26.21
had been cured of his leprosy or one of the skin diseases
called by that name. Cures were not uncommon; there
was even a law that a cured leper had to obtain a certificate
of good health; "Go, show thyself to your priest", he said Mk 1.44
to one. Simon may have been cured locally, but it is more
likely he had sought out the great Healer of Galilee, for

him he now invited to supper. The sharing of a meal was a close form of intimacy; that was why man dreamed of the Heavenly Banquet. But the meal was interrupted by a woman. That morning she had watched him mount an ass, accompanied by a small crowd, some with palm-branches. There went One greater than Judas the Hammer, and "Heaven bless you, King of the Jews", she said to herself and God. When he supped with Simon in the early evening, she entered the house and broke a flask of nard on his head. The harlot anointed his feet—sandals were not worn indoors—perhaps because she thought he was the Messiah's forerunner; this woman, breaking her alabaster flask of ointment on his head, believed he was the Messiah himself. The Indian ointment was costly, and there were murmurs about the waste; it might have been sold for a large sum of money and poor people relieved. He excused her, not because her action was what she intended, a regal anointing, but because it was the first of his funeral rites, an anointing of his body for burial. But he did not as on other occasions only say that his death would not be the end of the story. He went further, forecasting that the woman's funeral rite would cast its shadow, or rather its
Mk 14.9 light, over the whole world, "wheresoever the Gospel was preached".

According to St Mark it was on the journey to Jericho Mk 10.32f
that he spoke of all that the Son of Man must suffer, delivered to the chief priests and Gentiles, mocked, scourged and put to death; but it is more likely to have been later, perhaps on his first night in Jerusalem. He knew then that his appeal to people to see in him their true Messiah, "lowly and riding upon an ass", had been a tragic failure. In the woman's anointing he saw a funeral rite. But the "triumphal entry" had raised the disciples' hopes. James
and John asked that in his kingdom they might sit, one on Mk 10.35f
his right hand and the other on his left. "Ye know not what Mt 20.20f
ye ask", he said; "can ye drink of the cup that I drink of?" Of his cup of hemlock Socrates might have asked his friends the question, but he could not have gone on to ask, "or be baptized with the baptism that I am baptized withal?" At his first baptism the Holy Spirit descended from Heaven; at the new Baptism he himself would ascend to Heaven. Though the ten disciples knew that Salome was financing their pilgrimage, at least supplementing the alms dropped into Judas's money-bag, they were deeply offended by her son's request. Yet they were not much better themselves,
asking, "What shall we have?" He waved his hand to them Mt 19.27f
all: "Ye shall sit on twelve thrones judging the Twelve

Tribes of Israel." The words were mildly sarcastic, for there were not Twelve Tribes of Israel, only Two. More seriously
Mk 10.45 he said that the Son of Man had not come for self-glorification; he had come, not to be served, but to serve, to be a bondslave. A strange bondslave, who claimed the divine right to forgive sins and to abrogate the Mosaic Law! But he went further, "and to give life as a ransom for many". A bondslave whose death would be the purchase-money to set others free! He knew his death would be the means of bringing many into the Coming Kingdom, though its full import was still a mystery he could safely leave with his Heavenly Father. Meanwhile, knowing that in the morning he might be arrested by the Temple police, he opened his mind so far to the disciples. Wondering about his words, some of them lay awake for a long time that night. Yet they had settled down to sleep in the most secluded part of the Mount of Olives, the Garden of Gethsemane.

Lk 2.41f His mother told a strange story of his boyhood; taken to Jerusalem to be confirmed, he talked with members of the Sanhedrin, a religious tribunal and court of justice presided over by the High Priest. That was not impossible, for some members put themselves at the disposal of pilgrims to the Passover, answering questions. Gentile pilgrims were common; the forecourt of the Temple was called the Court of the Gentiles. For them it was natural to ask questions, but it seemed strange in the case of a Jewish boy brought to Jerusalem to be confirmed. As later in life he had a love for children and an affectionate interest in small creatures, such as sparrows, he may have questioned a rabbi about the lambs. Separated from the holier part of the Temple by a high wall, the Court of the Gentiles with its sacrificial animals sounded like a cattle-market. But louder in the Boy's ears than the lowing of cattle was the plaintive bleat-

ing of lambs. And when Joseph took him into the more
sacred part of the Temple, even beyond the Court of
Women to which his mother might have taken him, he
almost slipped on the blood of lambs. The Boy was not Jn 1.29
religious enough to approve of lambs being sacrificed. Yet
in the *Book of Revelation* he is pictured as a sacrificial lamb Rev 5.12
himself.

But Philip was wrong in telling the Ethiopian eunuch that Acts 8.32
He was dumb as a lamb before its shearer; he defied Isa 53.7
Caiaphas and the Sanhedrin by cleansing the Court of the
Gentiles. Though "Gentiles" means heathen, it was the one Mk 11.15f
Christian part of the Temple, fulfilling the prophetic words
in *Isaiah*, "Thy house shall be called a house of prayer for all Isa 56.7
nations". There Greeks and Romans could offer worship,
given glimpses through an open door of the High Altar,
almost of God himself. And it had its own sanctity; it
could not be used as a thoroughfare nor trodden by people Mk 11.16
with dust on their shoes. But busy traffic, the trade in
animals from cattle to pigeons, corn, wine, and incense, and
the exchange of Greek and Roman coins for Jewish shekels
with which they were bought, contaminated the whole
Temple. Though the traders and money-changers were
honest men, it was "a den of thieves", robbing God's
Temple of its sanctity. No pecuniary interest could com-
pensate for that loss. His popular entry into the city, though
felt as a failure, had invested him with a sense of responsibility. He was the Messenger foretold by the prophet: "he
shall purge the sons of Levi, and cleanse them as gold or Mal 3.3
silver is cleansed". Seizing an ox-goad he drove out the
cattle and sheep, knocking over the money-changers'
tables. The temple police could not interfere; he had the
sympathy or active support of a large number of pilgrims,

shocked by the Temple traffic. The police did not even stop urchins jumping about in their search for coins and
Mt 21.15 gleefully shouting, "Hosanna, Son of David". Of the Sadducees, the ecclesiastics, honourably named after Zadok, Solomon's High Priest, he made himself the enemy, and Pontius Pilate, the Roman Procurator, was their friend.

Later in the day, when he was teaching in the Temple,
Mk 11.27f some Sadducees asked him by what authority he had acted; he told them a parable, a strange parable in which he who
Mk 12.1f tells it is already dead. The *Wicked Husbandmen* is a con-
Isa 5.1f tinuation of Isaiah's *Song of the Vineyard.*

Isa 5.7 The Lord's vineyard is the house of Israel,
the men of Judah are his pleasant plantation.

He approved of the prophet's picture of Israel, expressing the Lord's care for his people, a vineyard set on a sunny hill, stones removed, protected from wild beasts by both wall and hedge, tower built for a watchman; planted with the choicest vines;

Isa 5.4 What more could he have done for his vineyard,
than that which he hath done?

Yet all failed;

Isa 5.2 He looked it should bring forth good grapes,
but, behold, it brought forth wildings.

The parable takes up the tale. The Lord of the vineyard sent servants to receive from the tenants the rent, part of the produce. Of these some were beaten and sent away empty, others were put to death. Perhaps the prophet Isaiah himself was one of the martyrs, tradition telling that his body was sawn asunder with a wooden saw; the last was John the Baptist, put to death by Herod. The Lord had one servant

left, the son whom he loved. "Him they will reverence" he said; but the tenants said, "This is the heir; come, let us kill him and the inheritance will be ours." Cast out of the vineyard, he was put to death. The Sadducees could not have failed to interpret the parable; he had cleared the Court of the Gentiles, claiming that as God's Son he had more authority than the six thousand priests on duty at the Passover. Yet he was a strange Son of God, foretelling in the parable he would be put to death. But to him it was not strange; he had come to regard his death as more valuable than his life. And his death would not be the end. In a sequel to the parable he quoted the proleptic words of the
psalmist: "The stone which the builders rejected, the same Mk 12.10
has become the head of the corner." Ps 118.22

On his way to the Mount of Olives that evening he turned to look back on the sacred city; with its Temple that, as Josephus said, appeared to strangers from a distance like a mountain covered with snow, the parts not gilt being
exceeding white, it was still in the words of Scripture, "the Ps 48.2
city of the Great King". Tears were in his eyes—"he wept" Lk 19.41
—as he broke out in a dirge in the old Hebrew style:

O Jerusalem, Jerusalem, Mt 23.37f

(he repeated the dear name, as he repeated the dear names, Martha, Martha, Simon, Simon)

Thou that slayest the prophets,
and stonest thy messengers,
How often have I longed

(it had become the dream of his life)

to gather thy children,
as a hen gathers her brood

(a vulture fluttering overhead)

under her wings,
and ye would not;
Behold, thy house is left thee
a desolation.

Mk 11.12f Returning to the city next morning, the disciples saw a
figtree he had cursed the day before; he had been hungry
and it had offered him no fruit; now it was withered to its
roots. But it had not been due to produce figs till June and it
was still April! St Luke, though he read it in St Mark, omits
this story of his unkindness to a helpless tree, while in *St*
Mt 21.19f *Matthew* there is a different version. Clearly a parable has
given rise to a miracle, the parable of the Barren Figtree.
In the Old Testament Israel is represented as a figtree: "I
Hos 9.10 saw your fathers as the first fruit on a figtree in her first
Lk 13.6f season." He kept the picture in the parable, a figtree
planted in a vineyard as an object of special cult and care.
Yet it was bearing no fruit. The landlord ordered the vine-
dresser to cut it down, but he pleaded that it might be
spared for another season in the hope that it might yet
produce fruit, and that was granted. This parable, in which
he spoke of his mission as a figtree, he had told in a synagogue in Galilee. If he remembered it, he would reflect
that months had passed without the fig tree showing much
promise of fruit. But there was still hope. The next two
days in Jerusalem, his last on earth, might be the figtree's
June.

It was still early morning when he began to teach in the
Jn 8.2 Temple "for all the people came early for to hear him".
But his teaching was interrupted. Pharisees were more
hostile than in the Galilean days; between them was a

widening gulf. To him they were too legal; they put
trivial obligations on the same level as obligations of a more
exalted character, such as showing charity to "publicans
and sinners". The Law itself was not without this fault; the
command "Thou shalt love thy neighbour as thyself" is Lev 19.18
immediately followed by the command, "Thou shalt not Lev 19.19
let a garment of mingled linen and wool come upon thee".
But the Pharisees could carry it too far; "they strained at a Mt 23.24
gnat and swallowed a camel". To them he was too illegal.
That people rested on the Sabbath even the Roman
Tacitus noticed, attributing it to Jewish indolence; but he
healed people on the Sabbath. He even regarded his
teaching as an addition to the Law; he was like a house-
holder "which bringeth out of his treasure things new and Mt 13.52
old". So some Pharisees interrupted his discourse in the
Temple, or more probably in its precincts, for they brought
with them a woman taken in adultery; they hoped to Jn 8.3f
catch him in a trap. According to *Deuteronomy* she was due Deut 22.22
to be stoned to death; what was his verdict? If he said she
should not be stoned, he was contravening the Law of
Moses; if he said she should be stoned, he could be charged
with arrogating to himself the peculiar right of the Roman
procurator. He bent down and wrote on the ground. If he
was following the practice of a Roman judge who, before
pronouncing sentence, wrote it down, what he wrote in the
dust can still be deciphered, for, raising his head, he said,
"Let him that is without sin cast the first stone". One by
one the Pharisees moved silently away. It is unlikely that
any of them had committed adultery, for Pharisees were
good-living men. Probably they were awed by his voice
and appearance, as was also the woman who addressed
him "Lord".

Unlike the Pharisees, the Sadducees belonged to old wealthy families, many of them priestly. In the parable
Lk 16.19f the *Rich Man and Lazarus* one character is clad in purple and fine linen, the outer garment dyed with the shell-fish murex, the inner made of Egyptian linen; the other character lies at his door desiring to be fed with crumbs that fell from the rich man's table; these represent the two classes in the land, the wealthy and the poor. Their disparity suggested the fanciful idea they were descended from two different Adams. There was no middle class; even the great Hillel followed a trade. Slaves come into several parables, called there servants. Most slaves were bought at Tyre or Sidon, but some were Jews sold to pay off a debt. He made no protest against slavery because, living in the houses of the wealthy, slaves might fare better than the independent poor, overtaxed on other things than salt and often out of work. With the poor, the hungry, the naked, and the debtors in prison he identified himself when he
Mt 25.45 said, "Inasmuch as ye did it unto one of the least of these my brethren, ye did it unto me". But he had no animosity against the wealthy; looking on the rich young ruler, "he
Mk 10.21 loved him". But he knew there was "a mammon of un-
Lk 16.9 righteousness"; its danger might be so serious that he said in his extravagant way, "It is easier for a camel to go through the eye of a needle than for a rich man to enter
Lk 18.25 the kingdom of Heaven". No doubt the Sadducees were offended by such a saying. But some were more offended by his cleansing of the Court of the Gentiles, its trade to them, being in charge of the Temple, a source of considerable revenue. But unlike the Pharisees they did not try to catch him in a dangerous trap. Friendly with Rome, under whose rule they felt their high position securer than it would be in the liberated Israel for which the Pharisees prayed, even offering in the Temple a daily sacrifice of an

ox and two lambs on behalf of the Roman emperor, they felt they could safely leave his fate to the procurator, Pilate. Meanwhile some Sadducees interviewed him to tell a story which, arguing with the Pharisees, they sometimes told to their own amusement.

The Sadducees were old-fashioned in their faith; of the Holy Scriptures, the Law, and the Prophets, edited by the scribes, they accepted only the first five books. These spoke of no future life, Adam having been barred from the Tree of Life by his obedience to the Serpent. So for the Sadducees souls went down to Sheol, a great cavern, ghosts with shadowy bodies. Arguing with the Pharisees they tried to make the Mk 12.18f
idea of a future life ridiculous with a story. A man died childless. According to the Law a brother had to marry the widow to raise for him an heir. Six brothers, one after the other, married the widow and all died childless. Last of all the woman died. Which of the seven brothers would be her husband in the new life, for they all had her? They smiled as the Pharisees appeared perplexed by the problem. But when they put it to him, he replied that they knew not the power of God. The new life was without the limited relations of the present life; it was like the life of angels, in which no such ridiculous situation as they imagined would arise. But he also told the Sadducees that they did not know their Scripture. God said to Moses in the story of the Burning Bush, "I am the God of Abraham, the Ex 3.1f
God of Isaac, and the God of Jacob". Moses was so impressed that he hid his face, afraid to look on God. He had imagined him as the God of Israel, but he had revealed himself as the personal God of the three patriarchs, of Abraham, of Isaac, and of Jacob. And "I am" he said, not "I was". He was not the God of the dead but of the living. The experience of God in the present life is the clear pointer to a future life with God.

The Sadducees gone, people would have gathered about him, but he waved them away and sat with eyes fixed on the Temple. He knew why the Sadducees had asked about a future life; they intended to bring his present life to an end. Yet he thought less of his own fate than of the fate of the city and, more important, the Holy Temple. He foresaw their destruction as Jeremiah had foreseen it six centuries before. The Temple destroyed! To them it was the centre of the world, its inner sanctuary, the Holy of Holies, the earth's navel. How secure it looked, the Roman fortress, Turris Antonia, overhanging a corner like a guardian. And there was its strength, some basic stones more than twenty cubits long. The great bronze door, the gift of a rich man, Nicanor, needed twenty men in the morning to push it open, the thunderous sound waking people in their beds. And all without and within, stones and woodwork, had been placed by priestly hands, though prepared by a large body of masons and carpenters.

Ps 11.3 If the foundations be destroyed,
what can the righteous do?

The psalmist almost equated it with heaven:

Ps 11.4 The Lord is in his holy temple,
the Lord's throne is in heaven.

Yet on entering the Temple that morning, he had not bought a cake and given it to a priest to be sacrificed, as Joseph had done when he was a boy. And if then he did not approve of the sacrifice of lambs, he was not reconciled to it now. And the sacrifice of larger animals, by which the priestly families greatly profited, had ceased to be a living and effective element in the faith of the worshippers; largely supported by Jews of the Dispersion unable to be present at a Passover, more numerous than the Palestinian Jews, it amounted to little more than a survival of the Law. And it was unlikely he approved of other cultic performances, such as dancing though a psalmist had said,

> Let them praise his name in the dance, Ps 149.3
> let them praise him with timbrel and harp.

He remembered the prophets: "I hate, I despise your feast Amos 5.21
days, and I will no more smell in your solemn assemblies",
said the Lord in *Amos*; and in *Isaiah*, "Bring no more vain Isa 1.13
oblations". If Jeremiah had prophesied the destruction of
the Temple because of the people's unfaithfulness to God,
he prophesied it for an even stronger reason: its priests
were about to put to death God's Son. Though the Emperor Titus pleaded that the Temple should be spared as
one of the world's wonders, it was destroyed. That was
about forty years later, but his vision of its destruction was
so strangely foreshortened that he told his disciples that he
would destroy it himself, and in three days raise a new Jn 2.19
Temple not made with hands. By the new Temple he Mt 26.61
meant the Kingdom of God, which was not made with
hands unless they were hands nailed to the Cross.

Next morning he did not go into the city, but sat viewing it Mt 24.3
from the Mount of Olives. The disciples stood apart in a
questioning group. He had said the coming of the Son of Man Mt 24.27
would be like lightning flashing from the east to the west;
that sounded not only sudden but almost immediate. The
Sadducees hostile, and also their opponents, the Pharisees,
the sky looked ominous, dark with thunder-clouds. He had
also said, "I am come to throw fire on the earth; would it Lk 12.49
were already kindled", and "I came not to send peace, but Mt 10.34
a sword". Was the catastrophic event, in which he would
be chief agent, about to take place? Peter, James, and John

the inner group of his disciples, the others asked to approach and question the silent Figure, taking with them
Mt 24.3f one of themselves, Andrew, Peter's brother. What these
asked of him was more or less what was asked later, the
perplexing, yet hopeful question, "Lord, wilt thou at this
Acts 1.6 time restore again the Kingdom to Israel?" His reply was
Mt 24.34 indefinite: "Verily, I say unto you, that this generation
shall not pass, till all these things be accomplished." When
they continued to look at him in a questioning way, he
Mt 24.35 said sharply, "Heaven and earth shall pass away, but my
words shall not pass away". Then after a pause, shaking
Mt 24.36 his head, he said: "Of that day and that hour knoweth no
man, no, nor the angels which are in heaven, neither the
Son, but the Father." Though he was higher than the
Angels, God's Son, yet incarnate he could not precisely
foretell a date. He had been wondering about the course
of events as he sat viewing the city, perhaps imagining
his death might coincide with the killing of lambs for the
Passover Supper. What he knew for certain was that his
death would be the birth of the Kingdom of God.

Yet there was the Cross! "Far be a cross not only from
the body, but from the thought, the eyes, the ears of a
Roman citizen." But he could not dismiss it from his mind
like Cicero; the Figure on his Cross was staring him in the
Deut 21.23 face. But "he that is hanged is accursed of God", said the
Law; and to be nailed to a cross, a cruel Roman gallows,
was worse than to be hung from a tree. Could he be so
accursed of God? He had made Satan in the wilderness call
Mt 4.3 him "Son of God". To the disciples he had spoken of him-
Mt 9.15 self as the Bridegroom, though God in Scripture was the
Isa 54.5 Husband of Israel. "Holy Father" in the *Fourth Gospel* is a
Jer 31.32 mistake; he never so addressed God; it implied a distance
Jn 17.11 he did not feel. "Many prophets and kings desired to see
Lk 10.24 what ye see and did not see it", he said to his disciples;

"a greater than Jonah is here", "a greater than Solomon", Mt 12.41–2
"in this place is one greater than the temple". It seemed Mt 12.6
almost blasphemous to think God would suffer his Son to
be put to a cruel and shameful death. But he thought of the
things he had said of his death, as "a ransom for many". Mt 20.28
He may even have remembered saying, "not a sparrow Mt 10.29
falls to the ground without the Father's knowledge".
What could his death mean but the last and greatest revelation of God's love for a sinful world, the sacrifice of his Son? It would not be propitiatory like a sacrifice in the Temple; that the innocent should suffer for the guilty was not a moral idea. God's merciful love for sinners would not be the result of the Cross, but its cause and source.

Joining the disciples, he sent Judas as their steward to buy food in the city. Perhaps he entered it by the Fish Gate, meat the daily diet only of the rich. Judas gone, he spoke more freely about the suffering Son of Man and his coming again in glory. That he did forecast a physical resurrection is clear from the disillusionment and dismay the disciples were to feel. Yet, above all, he told them to have faith.
That had been a main theme of his teaching, and he had
spoken of it with a poetical extravagance. "If ye had faith Lk 17.6
as a grain of mustard seed"—the smallest of all seeds—
"ye might say unto this sycamine tree, Be thou plucked up by the root, and be thou planted in the sea; and it should obey you." Peter, James, and John, fishermen, could not imagine a sycamine tree growing in the Sea of Galilee; their faith was less than a grain of mustard seed that Friday afternoon.

The friend who lent him the ass on which he rode into Jerusalem may have been one of his patients; his reputation as a healer widespread, they had come from all parts,

Simon the Leper from Bethany. In that case a fatal relapse
later might account for the fact that we do not know his
Acts 12.12 name, though we know his wife's name, Mary. Only a
person of some wealth possessed an ass; perhaps he had
made his money by trading with the Romans, for to his
son's Jewish name, John, he added a Roman name, Mark.
His house was in the richer part of the city; it had a small
Acts 12.13 courtyard with a gate, attended by a slave-girl, Rhoda.
Mk 14.12f It had also what was unusual, a large upper chamber. He
sent word, perhaps through Mark, that there he and his
disciples might hold the Passover Supper; also the Kiddush.

Lk 22.8 Peter and John he sent to the city with instructions.
From the Mount of Olives they would enter it by the Valley Gate, much used by water-carriers, as nearby was one of the city's wells. They would see a young man carrying a water-jar, an unusual sight; women as a rule went to a well; a water-jar balanced on head or shoulder gave them a graceful carriage. That he would recognize them makes it likely he was Mark, playing the part of a slave. They would follow him as, conspicuous with his water-jar, he made his way up the crowded street of the Valley of Cheese-makers, and then by side lanes reached a large house. To them the door would be opened by a slave-girl. All passed as planned, the secrecy saving the operation from the watchful eyes of the Temple police. The chamber was prepared, couches placed about a long table, on which were set loaves of unleavened bread, round and crusty, and a flask of red wine; also a bowl of spiced vinegar, into which bread and bitter herbs could be dipped. The Paschal lamb would be bought on the following day, having been sacrificed in the Temple. It would be partaken of after sunset, when a new day began, a Friday. Food for the Kiddush was also provided. That Rhoda, the slave-girl, helped with the preparations, fetching one thing and another, is likely.

It would begin her interest in the great apostle, whose
voice at the door some years later she was so glad to hear Acts 12.12f
that she forgot to open it, but ran and told her mistress,
Mary, and others in the house, that Peter was out of prison.

As the spring day grew dusk, he and his disciples made their
way, probably their devious ways, to the friend's house.
There they partook of the Kiddush, the Sanctification,
a religious meal preceding a solemn occasion, in this
case the Passover Supper. They did not sit on stools
as at an ordinary meal, but reclined on the prepared
couches. The Kiddush ended, he said, "With desire I Lk 22.15
have desired to eat the Passover with you before I
suffer". It was a family meal, but he and his disciples
were a family. He knew his great desire might be
thwarted by the Temple police. He told the disciples that
one of them would betray him. They looked at one another
in a wondering, even unbelieving way; had he not said that
his twelve disciples would sit on twelve thrones in his
Kingdom? But he had been studying Judas. On his entry
into the city Judas had not cried "Hosanna" like other
disciples. *The Parable of the Wicked Husbandmen,* in which Mk 12.1f
the landlord's son is put to death, had aroused in him an
alert interest. When he returned from the fish-market that
day, he had a covert look on his face, as though he had been
on some private mission. And now, when he spoke of his
great desire to eat the Passover with his disciples, he read
in Judas' raised eyebrows the question, "Was this all they
had come to Jerusalem for, to eat a Passover Supper?" In Mk 14.18
speaking of a traitor without giving his name, he made a
last appeal to Judas. He felt a pity for him; how he had
disappointed his hopes in not being the patriotic rebel he
expected. He could only sadly say, "Good were it for that Mk 14.21

Jn 13.29 man had he not been born". Even when Judas left the
room, the disciples merely imagined their steward had
gone to find a small market still open to supply bread and
spring vegetables for their late supper on the Mount of
Jn 13.30 Olives. The poetic *Fourth Gospel* gives a more dramatic
account of his departure: "Judas went out, and it was night."

Judas gone, he would have a last supper with his disciples,
a Death-feast; but it would not be on the Mount of Olives.
He took the loaf of unleavened bread and the flask of red
wine, set apart for the Passover Supper; of that meal
neither he nor his disciples would partake. His death had
Mt 26.24 been predicted: "The Son of Man goeth even as it is written
of him." If his death was his Father's will he would make
it his own will. Breaking the bread, he passed it to his disciples. Gifts are not given with a frown, but with a smile, and there was at least a kindly look in his eyes as he said, "This is my body given for you". But love asks for love in return, and he added, "This do in remembrance of me". The red wine he poured into a cup and passing it round gave thanks. A painful death on a cross is the strangest thing for which a person ever gave thanks. He explained its
meaning: "This cup is the new covenant in my blood."
Ex 24.1–8 The Old Covenant, between God and Israel, had been
ratified on Mount Sinai by the blood of oxen, part shed on
the altar, part sprinkled on the priests. Israel had been
unfaithful to that Covenant, and Jeremiah had foretold a
Jer 31.31–3 New Covenant, a new order of things established not on
stone but in the hearts of men. But he was so far from foreseeing what would ratify that New Covenant he can hardly be called its prophet; it would be ratified by the human blood of God's incarnate Son.

The bread had no existential oneness with his body, as was later believed, his body being still alive. Nor was his death a sacrifice to reconcile God to men; on the contrary

"God so loved the world that he gave his Son". The idea of Jn 3.16
a change being effected in God is a contradiction of his
eternal nature. St Paul expresses the ministry of reconcilia-
tion, "to wit, God was in Christ reconciling the world unto 2 Cor 5.19,20
himself". "Be ye reconciled to God", he says. The *Parable
of the Prodigal Son* washes away all thought of God being
reconciled: "when he was yet a great way off, his father Lk 15.20
saw him, and ran, and fell on his neck, and kissed him".

The singing of a psalm in the upper chamber roused the young man, Mark. His father's guests, especially the One who was a prophet and more than a prophet had excited his interest, and he lay listening. When he heard steps on the stair, he sprang out of bed and, not taking time to don a tunic, followed them to the door. He opened it after them and saw the Prophet and his friends standing in the moonlit courtyard. He drew the door close, yet left space
enough to see them and overhear what was said. "When I Lk 22.35–6
sent you without purse, or scrip, lacked ye anything?" "Nothing", they replied. "But now, he that hath a purse, let him take it, and likewise his scrip; and he that hath no sword, let him sell his garment and buy one." The

disciples stood in silent amazement. Then one of them,
perhaps Simon the Zealot, said, "Lord, behold, here are two
Lk 22.38 swords". "Enough, enough", he said. His disciples did not
understand his strange way of saying for the sake of emphasis almost the opposite of what he meant. Mark was so surprised himself that he decided to follow this strange prophet though with only a sheet about his body on an April night. He was a strange prophet, stranger than Mark realized, thinking more of the inhospitality his disciples would meet with than its cause, their Master's shameful death on a cross.

Mk 14.26f Passing through the gate, the party broke up to go by
different ways to their common destination. He knew it was his father's orchard on the Mount of Olives, Gethsemane. Clad in his sheet, he hastened down a dark lane and, leaving the city by the Water Gate, crossed the Kidron and ascended the slope. Seeking shelter in the shade of a tree, he watched the party reassemble. All was clear by the light of the full Passover moon. The gate was opened and the Prophet with three disciples, one of them Peter, entered the orchard; the others remained outside sitting on the ground or leaning against the wall. As *St Mark's Gospel* shows a peculiar interest in Peter, relating almost trivial things, no doubt it was from the Apostle that Mark heard what happened in the Garden of Gethsemane.

His practice was always to pray by himself, perhaps on a hillside by night, his relation to God unique; this night
he sought the sympathetic fellowship of his three favourite
Mk 14.34f disciples. "My soul is exceeding sorrowful unto death; stay
you here and watch." Moving apart, he flung himself on the ground. There was silence for a time; then it was broken by the cry, "Father, take away this cup". To the disciples the cry was sad, yet strange; had he not passed round the cup an hour ago at their last supper? "They wist

not what to say to him." Then after a long pause he said in a lowered voice, "Yet not what I will, but what thou wilt." A long silence followed and the disciples settled down as though to sleep. But he continued to lie in prayer. He would not have been human, if he had not shrunk from the pain of a cross, and also its shame; it would be conspicuous to people on the highway. He lay for a long time; then, rising, he came to his disciples and, finding them half asleep, said with a gentle reproach, "Could you not watch with me one hour?" Again he flung himself on the ground, but when he rose and came a second time, "Sleep on now, and take your rest", he said. He did not feel the need of their sympathy with the full acceptance of his Father's will.

Voices were approaching, and lights under the trees. The other disciples slipped away quietly; Peter, James, and John he led to the orchard gate. There they were faced by a small crowd, armed with swords and clubs, the Temple police. It was for a mob they were so prepared. The passover had brought thousands of pilgrims to Jerusalem and many of them regarded him as a great prophet, if not the Messiah himself. An open arrest might have caused an uprising. The Sadducees had sought to guard against that by accepting the offer of Judas to guide the police to where he could be quietly arrested, a private orchard. Yet it was on the slope of the Mount of Olives, where most of the pilgrims encamped at night, and as a precaution the police were provided with arms. They did not need to have him pointed out; most of them were familiar with the Figure who had caused a commotion by his entry into the city or by his cleansing the Court of the Gentiles. But Judas had made the request that he might approach him and kiss his hand, the customary way a disciple greeted a Rabbi. That he accepted only a small sum

Ex 21.32 for the betrayal, thirty pieces of silver, the legal fine for
injury done to a slave, suggests his motive was not money.
Had he no hope of forcing the hand he kissed? Might it not
act in some miraculous way, the hand of the Messiah? So
his Master interpreted the questioning kiss, a last appeal of
Judas. Instead of snatching away his hand he said, "Com-
rade, wherefore art thou come?" When the three disciples
saw their Master seized and bound, powerless to help and
themselves viewed with threatening looks, they fled. As
the police moved away with their Prisoner, one of them
saw under an olive tree something brighter than the
leaves shimmering in the moonshine. He sprang forward
and seized it, a white linen sheet; the owner, a young man,
slipping out of it, had started to run down the hill. As none
Mk 14.51–2 of the disciples witnessed the incident except Judas, soon
to commit repentant suicide, it could have been reported
by no one but the young man himself. He reported it about
thirty years later when he wrote the earliest Life of Jesus,
the *Gospel according to St Mark.* As writings at that time
were anonymous, or ascribed to such personages as Enoch
and Solomon, his report of the trivial incident, not taken
up by St Matthew or St Luke, may be regarded as the
author's signature to his Gospel.

Mk 14.53 The hour too late for a meeting of the Sanhedrin, he was
taken to the palace of the high Priest and questioned by his
father-in-law Annas, a former High Priest. He was not easy
to question, careful not to commit himself. "Is it lawful to
Mk 12.14f give tribute to Caesar?" he had been asked. "Yes" would
have lost him his popularity with the people; "No" would
have endangered him with Rome. Pointing to the Emperor's image on a coin, he said, "Render unto Caesar the
things that are Caesar's", a reply that meant little or

nothing more than that the matter was not his personal concern. His concern was with themselves, made in God's image, and "Render to God the things that are God's", he added. But though questioning was difficult, Annas felt he admitted enough for a formal trial in the morning. He handed him to two policemen to be taken to the fortress, Antonia; there, an alleged rebel against Rome, he would be safely guarded through the night.

In the courtyard of the palace was a group of people
gathered round a brazier-fire. A slave-girl, pointing to a
man, cried to the others, "This is one of them", and to the
man, "You, too, are a Nazarene". The man was Peter. As
the policemen led the Prisoner away, he heard Peter calling
down curses on his head if he knew the man. Peter was a
strange rock on which to build a Church! Yet he was the
only disciple who had followed the police into the city;
also, he confessed to the others, who would not otherwise
have known it, that he had shamefully denied his Master.
"Peter wept bitterly." Lk 22.62

Early in the morning he was taken to the Temple, where
in a court adjoining the Court of Women the Sanhedrin had
been hastily convened, Caiaphas himself presiding. Not all
its seventy members, Sadducees, Pharisees, and scribes,
would be present at such an hour, but one of them, Joseph of
Arimathea, reported what took place. The charge against
him was that he had said he would destroy the Temple Mk 14.58
made with hands and in three days build a Temple not
made with hands. That sounded like sacrilege; Caiaphas
raised his eyes to heaven and quoted, "O holy and beautiful Isa 64.11
house, where our fathers praised thee". It might be con- Lev 24.16
sidered blasphemy, and according to the Law, "He that
blasphemeth shall surely be put to death". He could not
sentence him to crucifixion, a Roman privilege introduced
for political offenders, but he could to stoning, the fate of

the first Christian martyr, Stephen. But stoning might
excite his sympathizers more than a public arrest, which
the Sadducees had avoided. Caiaphas felt he could safely
Mk 15.1f leave the matter to Pilate; to him he would allege that he
Mk 15.6 claimed to be the Messiah, King of the Jews. A false Messiah, Barabbas, who had caused an insurrection, was
waiting in prison for his crucifixion. Pilate kept him waiting, for it was his custom to placate the Jews by releasing a
Mk 14.61–2 condemned prisoner at the Passover. "Art thou the Messiah?" Caiaphas asked his Prisoner, and the reply was "I
am". It was not a strong affirmation, but a qualified assent,
"I am, if you choose to give me that title". Then quoting
Ps 110.1 from the *Coronation Psalm* and *Daniel*, he went on, "and
Dan 7.13 henceforth ye shall see the Son of Man sitting on the right
hand of power and coming in the clouds of heaven". To
say Caiaphas would see it was only a manner of speaking.
His coming would not be a descending to earth again, but
an ascending to heaven, a triumph over death and an
Ex 3.14 exaltation to his Father. But the "I am" of the poetical
statement was plain enough prose for the High Priest's
purpose. How distressed he was to hand over his Prisoner
to Pilate he displayed by the mock sign of rending his
garment. It could have been a costly gesture, for a High
Ex 28.31–4 Priest's robe, seamless and blue, was fringed with silver
bells and an appendage that looked like pomegranates.
The bells tinkled as he rose and left the court.

Caiaphas asked Pilate for an immediate trial. The pilgrims, Galileans and others, who had shouted "Hosanna", would not yet have left the Mount of Olives; there could be no disturbance. All would be over before the Passover Supper, the crucifixion taking place while the lambs were being sacrificed in the Temple. Friendly with Caiaphas and the other Sadducees who supported him, Pilate granted his request.

From the Hall of Cut Stones in the Temple he was taken to Jn 18.28f
the Praetorium, Herod's palace and Pilate's official resi-
dence during the Passover. A heathen building, a Jew
would not enter it for fear of defilement, and the judge's
chair was brought from it and placed on the wide pave-
ment outside. The charge against the Accused was what
Caiaphas suggested, his claim to be the Messiah; yet it was
different, sacrilegious in one case and in the other anarchic.
"Art thou the King of the Jews?" Pilate asked; the reply was Mk 15.2
ambiguous, "Thou sayest it". By a plain "Yes" he would
have compelled Pilate to take action, and while he knew
his death was the purpose of his life, he would do nothing
to hasten it, leaving all to the working will of his Father.
Pilate was a cruel man, as Philo and Josephus tell; some
harmless pilgrims to the Passover he had put to death,
"mingling their blood with the blood of the sacrifice"; Lk 13.1
a few years later he suppressed a Samaritan disturbance
with such excessive cruelty that he was recalled to Rome;
but he did not care to be treated by Caiaphas as though he
were a fool. This prisoner did not look like the Messiah, a
revolutionary king. But he saw a way out of his dilemma;
he offered to release him as his Passover gift. This caused Jn 18.39f
an outcry, "Crucify him, crucify him". It came from a
crowd that the Sadducees, priests, and scribes, had hastily
collected, people attached to the Temple he had purged
and insulted. The call was for the release of Barabbas as
Pilate's Passover gift. Staying in the palace was Herod
Antipas, tetrarch of Galilee; though not strictly a Jew, he
had come to Jerusalem for the Passover. Hearing the accused was a Galilean, Pilate sent him to Herod. The tetrarch, instigated by Herodias, a divorced niece he had
divorced his wife to marry, had put John the Baptist to
death, and in this greater Galilean prophet he was interested. Glad of the interview, he asked him many questions, Lk 23.6–12

but to all the answer was a majestic silence. Herod gave his
judgement of this King of the Jews by sending him back
arrayed in a pretentious garment that looked like a royal
robe; Pilate would enjoy the deadly jest. Yielding to the
Mk 15.15 cries, "Crucify him, crucify him", Pilate released Barabbas.

The trial ended, The Prisoner was scourged on the back
with a bunch of whips weighted with bits of metal or bone.
Then escorted by four Roman soldiers, the usual quarter-
nion, he began the slow walk to his life's destination, a
Mk 15.22 small hill called Calvary or in Aramaic, Golgotha, the
Skull. Near the North Road it attracted the attention of
travellers by its likeness to a skull; perhaps it was a skull,
Adam's, Jerusalem being built on his grave. But wooden
posts about eight feet tall also drew the attention of travellers; they were the uprights of crosses. That Calvary was
outside the city wall have may been in his mind when in
Mk 12.8 the *Parable of the Wicked Husbandmen* he said he was cast out
of the vineyard and put to death.

News of the trial had spread through the city and there
was an accompanying crowd. He stopped at the sight of
some weeping women, not of his acquaintance, for "Daugh-
Lk 23.27f ters of Jerusalem" he addressed them. They were not
weeping for what for them was impossible, their Messiah
on his way to be crucified; the crown of thorns that had
been placed on his head did not suggest the King of the
Jews. It was one more case of his attraction for women,
this time by the sad nobility of his appearance. Only the
sound of wailing could have withdrawn him from his deep
private thoughts. But these thoughts were less for himself
than for the fate that could not fail to fall on Jerusalem.
"Weep not for me, but for yourselves and for your children." His death on a cross needed no pity, as though it

were without a divine meaning and not illuminated by a heavenly glory.

Scourging, the preliminary of the cross, sometimes saved a man from the cross, causing an earlier death. This time it caused the stumbling of a strong body that for a year or more had been walking in all weathers the rough roads of Palestine. He could no longer carry on his shoulders the transverse beam of the cross. None of the Roman soldiers would have carried anything so shameful. They looked around, but the crowd shrank back, among them Barabbas who, released from Antonia, had hurried to see the end of his rival Messiah. The soldiers halted a man coming from the opposite direction; the Jerusalem crowd would
not protest at the shameful burden being laid on a stranger Mk 15.21
from the country. Yet he was not an entire stranger; though he had left his wife and children in Africa, he had come to Jerusalem to partake of the Passover Supper with relations. That he waited to watch the Crucifixion is likely, for his name came to be known. And his sons, Alexander and Rufus, became Christians; also their mother, for whom St Paul had a great affection. Probably it was Simon of Cyrene who reported the words, *ipsissima verba*, spoken from the Cross.

His naked body was laid on a level cross, hands nailed to its arms, strange arms for such healing hands. Then the cross was hoisted into its socket. Two brigands were crucified with him, he in the middle, as suited the accusing title fastened over his head, "King of the Jews". They were a remarkable trinity. In Jerusalem was a Society of Friends, whose members attended crucifixions and gave sufferers a cup of drugged wine, the soldiers not interfering. He re-
fused the cup, perhaps remembering, "I will not drink Mt 26.29

henceforth of this fruit of the vine until that day when
I drink it new with you in my Father's Kingdom".
Mk 15.29 Some of the crowd mocked him: "Thou that destroyest
the temple, and buildest it in three days, save thyself."
Lk 23.34 But it was them he wanted to save: "Father, forgive them,
Mt 5.44 for they know not what they do." "Love your enemies"
must have seemed an impossible counsel, but he was true
to his own teaching, even on the Cross. Perhaps that was
what made a centurion, probably a Gentile serving under
Mk 15.39 Herod, say, "Truly this man was the Son of God". Even one
of the brigands, though in cruel pain, was so inspired with
Lk 23.42f faith in his fellow-sufferer that he said, "Lord, remember
me when thou comest into thy Kingdom". Even on the
Cross he answered him in his poetic way, "Today shalt
thou be with me in paradise". They would eat together of
the Tree of Life in God's Garden. Perhaps the six hours,
three before noon and three after, were drawing to an end,
when with a loud voice he uttered the cry, "My God, my
Mk 15.34 God, why hast thou forsaken me?" That the words are in
Hebrew, not in the spoken Aramaic, shows they are a
Ps 22.1 quotation, the opening words of the *Twenty-second Psalm*.
It was the only occasion he said, "My God"; even in the
Garden of Gethsemane it was "My Father". And when he
Lk 23.46 quoted another psalm, "Into thy hands I commend my
Ps 31.5 spirit", he added the "Father". How he, "meek and lowly
Mt 11.29 in heart", came to know he was God's Son, it would be
pointless to ask, for, if he was, he could not have been
ignorant of it. That it was with a loud voice he cried, "It is
Jn 19.30 finished" suggests a sense of triumph. Perhaps it was less
of his Crucifixion he was thinking than of his Incarnate
career. It was so finished that of the dead and derelict
1 Cor 1.24 Figure on the Cross St Paul could say, "Christ crucified . . .
the power of God and the wisdom of God", the strange seal
of God's omnipotence and answer to all men's questions.

All four evangelists say, "He gave up the ghost". They were thinking, not of his parting breath, but of the release of his spirit; he had accepted the limits of a human life; that ended, his spirit would rise to a higher life. St Luke in
the *Acts of the Apostles* speaks of his Gospel as an account of Acts 1.1
all "he began to do and teach". St Mark gives as the title to his Gospel, "The beginning of the Gospel of Jesus Christ", meaning by Gospel, not a book, but the proclamation of good news. In this case it was God's proclamation through his Son, and of that his Son's life had been only a beginning. St Paul could not have been mainly interested
in that life when he said, "Yea, though we have known 2 Cor 5.16
Christ after the flesh, know we him no more". His main interest was in the Crucifixion and the love of God it revealed, and in the risen Christ.

Crucified bodies were buried naked in the earth; in this Mk 15.43
case Joseph of Arimathaea begged the body of Pilate, and it was granted. Wrapt according to custom in strips of blue linen, it was laid in a rock-hewn tomb, Joseph's own prospective tomb. Against its opening was rolled in a groove in the rock a heavy round stone like a great millstone. The body would be safe from jackals by night.

The earliest story of the Resurrection is in the earliest Gospel, *St Mark*. Returning from Calvary that afternoon, Mary Magdalene and two other women prepared spikenard and ointment to anoint the body. They rested on the
Saturday, their Sabbath, but early on the Sunday, the Mk 16.1f
Christian Sabbath, they made their way to the sepulchre. But "Who will roll us away the stone?" they asked. But they found the stone already rolled back. They also saw in the tomb a young man clothed in a long white garment, who told them, "He is not here, he is risen". If the young

man was not what the frightened women imagined, a heavenly being, but Mark, who had risen earlier than they had and cast about his body a white sheet, there could be no better authenticated story of the physical Resurrection.

Jn 21.1f The latest story is in the latest Gospel, *St John*. "I go a-fishing", said Peter, and "We go with thee", said the other disciples. Though they fished throughout the night, they caught nothing. In the morning they saw a figure on the shore, but did not recognize in him their resurrected Master. He told them to cast their net on the other side of the boat, and when they did so they could not draw it in for the multitude of fishes. When at last it was brought to land, it was found to be full of great fishes, an hundred and fifty and three. The story is symbolic. The disciples' desire to go a-fishing was their desire to proclaim the Gospel. That they fished in the dark and from the wrong side of the boat and caught nothing was their vain preaching to the hostile Jews. Morning, the right side of the boat, and the multitude of fishes speak of their successful preaching to the Gentiles. Even the number, one hundred and fifty and three, is symbolic, for according to the zoologist, Opianus Cilix, that was the total number of fish in the sea. Their proclaiming the Gospel would draw men of all nations.

The strongest evidence for the Risen Christ comes from St Paul; that is strange and convincing, for he hated the Christians. What happened on his way to Damascus to
Acts 9.3f persecute them he told St Luke, who was for a time his medical attendant, and he reports what he was told. He saw a great light and heard a voice, "Saul, Saul, why persecutest thou me?" The light was an inward illumination; one does not see a great light on a sunlit desert road. Of the

voice St Luke says some of the company heard it, the others
not. But the others were not deaf and an audible voice
they would have heard; clearly the voice was private to
Paul. It sounds like the voice of the Risen Christ. There is
the characteristic repetition of the name, "Saul, Saul";
and "Why persecutest thou me?" the speaker identifying
himself with the persecuted Christians, has a strong
resemblance to the saying, "inasmuch as ye did it unto one Mt 25.40
of the least of these my brethren, ye did it unto me." Even
more direct than the report through St Luke is what St Paul
himself says in an Epistle, "It pleased God . . . to reveal his Gal 1.15,16
Son in me, that I might preach him among the heathen".
And how faithful he was to that revelation; "I was not dis-
obedient unto the heavenly vision", he said to King Acts 26.19
Agrippa, and under the Emperor Nero he suffered martyr-
dom. In later life he had experiences of a kind called
mystical: "I was caught up into paradise, and heard un- 2 Cor 12.4
speakable words"; but to these he attached little or no
importance compared with his factual experience on the
road to Damascus.

St Paul spoke of himself as "one born out of season"; 1 Cor 15.8
but he did not mean he was an abortion; on the contrary
he had been born too late, three years after the other
apostles. Of these the first was St Peter, from whom he Lk 24.34
heard the story, for they were good friends before they 1 Cor 15.5
quarrelled. There is no record of it in the Gospels; it may
have been in the Gospel of his friend, St Mark, but the end
of that Gospel is lost. That Peter was the first to receive a
revelation may seem strange, for the last his Master saw or
heard of him was his denying all knowledge of him to a
slave-girl; yet that is almost what we might expect of
of Jesus. The encounter was so real to St Peter that forty
days later, at Pentecost, he risked imprisonment, even
stoning to death, by proclaiming the gospel in Jerusalem.

1 Cor 15.5f St Paul tells that the next revelation came to all twelve
disciples; the report sounds true, because it is slightly
inaccurate; Judas gone, there were eleven disciples. Then
St Paul says he revealed himself to a large body of brethren
"many of them still alive", he adds, as though suggesting
that the Corinthians might hear the story for themselves.
He speaks of no revelation to a woman, not even to Mary
Magdalene. That would not surprise the Corinthians, told
1 Cor 11.3 "the head of the woman is the man"; but it might have
surprised the Galatians told later, "In Christ Jesus is neither
Gal 3.28 male nor female". St Paul makes a point of telling that he
1 Cor 15.7 revealed himself to his eldest brother, James. In Nazareth
Mk 3.21,31 James believed his brother was not in his right mind; in
Acts 12.17 Jerusalem he became the head of the Church, James the
Gal 1.19 Just, and was stoned to death thirty years later. Mary, his
Gal 2.9, 12 mother, was also converted; so, too, were the other bro-
Acts 1.14 thers, for we read of them, Mary also present, gathered
with the apostles in the upper chamber in Jerusalem,
where he instituted the Last Supper. When St Paul speaks
of his own case, the last, he says he does not deserve to be
1 Cor 15.9, 10 called an apostle, having persecuted the Church of God; of
all the apostles he is the least. That he adds, "but I laboured
more abundantly than them all", sounds a little boastful;
yet it helps us to realize how vital had been his experience
on the way to Damascus.

But the experience of others, more or less disciples, was
Mk 14.27 as dramatic. Though he quoted the prophecy of the
Zech 13.7 shepherd being smitten and the sheep scattered, they were
dismayed by what had happened. Like the two men who,
turning their backs on Jerusalem, walked to Emmaus, they
Lk 24.21 had trusted "that it had been he which should have re-
deemed Israel", and were disappointed, sorrowful, and
without hope. Then something happened which changed
them into a jubilant company ready to risk their lives to

proclaim their renewed and richer faith. If they had not been seriously convinced of the actuality of the Resurrection, there would have been no Gospel to preach and no Church. The Cross itself they saw in a new light; its lonely victim had not been defeated, but had triumphed over death. Yet he had not been lonely; he had been God's revelation of himself to a sinful world, the proof of that the Resurrection. And the Divine presence, of which they had been partly aware in their Master, was with them still and in a deeper and more intimate way. He had rightly said
that it was expedient that he should go from them that he Jn 16.7
might come again; he had come again in the Risen Christ.
As news of the Resurrection spread—"this thing was not Acts 26.26
done in a corner"—it created an excitement that even the Roman historian Tacitus noticed, though he spoke of it as a mischievous superstition.

Countless Christians have shared the experience of the Risen Christ, for in the spiritual Gospel, *St John*, he is identified with the Paraclete, the Holy Ghost. And for St Paul
they are two in one: "I live, yet not I, but Christ liveth in Gal 2.20
me"; "Now the Lord is that Spirit". And this is in accord 2 Cor 3.17
with the prophetic teaching of the historic Jesus himself. He never spoke of reappearing as a ghost, still less with a
body that could eat broiled fish and pass through a closed Lk 24.42
door, as the Gospels record; he would come again in glory. Jn 20.19
The Risen Christ is one with the Holy Ghost, an *alter ego*, yet different. The difference is partly a matter of words and of people's point of view. Christians at the Eucharist, kneeling before the Crucifix, pray to the Risen Christ; on more ordinary occasions they pray for the guidance or inspiration of the Holy Spirit. Yet at both times they feel they are praying to God. This implies the Doctrine of the Trinity, not one Individual nor three Individuals, but a personal unity existing eternally in three eternal modes or

functions. It is not a mathematical absurdity or even a theological problem; it means that if God is love, there exists within his being an internal relationship which alone makes love possible. The words, "the Father, the Son, and the Holy Ghost" are less something we understand than a heavenly harmony we hear.